Alpha
Cat

On the cover
A for *American Curl*
C for *Ceylon*

Graphic design and layout
Paola Gallerani

Editorial assistant
Serena Solla

Translation
Catherine Bolton

Editing
Yarwood Editorial Services

Color separation
Eurofotolit, Cernusco sul Naviglio, Milano

Printed by
Graphicom, Vicenza

Grateful acknowledgement is made for permission to reprint short passages from the following works: *Particularly Cats ... And Rufus* by Doris Lessing © A. Knopf 1991; *A Cat Abroad: The Further Adventures of Norton, the Cat Who Went to Paris, and His Human* by Peter Gethers © Fawcett Columbine 1993; *A Dictionary of Cat Lovers: XV Century B.C. XX Century A.D.* by Christabel Aberconway © Michael Joseph, 1968; Vikki Myron, "Dewey's Guide for Library Cats," in Sandra Choron, Harry Choron and Arden Moore, *Planet Cat. A Cat-alog*, ©Houghton Mifflin 2007; "The Naming of Cats" by T.S. Eliot © Houghton Mifflin and © Faber and Faber 1939

isbn: 978-88-97737-17-9
© Officina Libraria, Milan, 2013
© Paola Gallerani (text), 2013
© Gabriella Gallerani (illustrations), 2013

Officina Libraria
via Carlo Romussi 4
20125 Milan, Italy
www.officinalibraria.com

Printed in Italy

Gabriella Gallerani *original drawings*

Paola Gallerani *text*

Alpha

Cat

**OFFICINA
LIBRARIA**

The Naming of Cats

The Naming of Cats is a difficult matter,
It isn't just one of your holiday games;
You may think at first I'm as mad as a hatter
When I tell you, a cat must have THREE DIFFERENT NAMES.

First of all, there's the name that the family use daily,
Such as Peter, Augustus, Alonzo or James,
Such as Victor or Jonathan, George or Bill Bailey -
All of them sensible everyday names.

There are fancier names if you think they sound sweeter,
Some for the gentlemen, some for the dames:
Such as Plato, Admetus, Electra, Demeter -
But all of them sensible everyday names.

But I tell you, a cat needs a name that's particular,
A name that's peculiar, and more dignified,
Else how can he keep his tail perpendicular,
Or spread out his whiskers, or cherish his pride?

Of names of this kind, I can give you a quorum,
Such as Munkustrap, Quaxo, or Coricopat,
Such as Bombalurina, or else Jellylorum -
Names that never belong to more than one cat.

But above and beyond there's still one name left over,
And that is the name that you never will guess;
The name that no human research can discover -
But THE CAT HIMSELF KNOWS, and will never confess.

When you notice a cat in profound meditation,
The reason, I tell you, is always the same:
His mind is engaged in a rapt contemplation
Of the thought, of the thought, of the thought of his name:
His ineffable effable
Effanineffable
Deep and inscrutable singular NAME.

T. S. Eliot, *Old Possum's Book of Practical Cats*, London: Faber & Faber, 1939.

The Naming of a Cat

That naming a cat is a serious business was evident well before T. S. Eliot devoted one of the masterpieces of twentieth-century poetry to the issue.

In papyrus from the *Book of the Dead* of Nebseni at the British Museum in London, datable to Dynasty XVIII of Ancient Egypt (which includes the reigns of the pharaohs Hatshepsut and Tutankhamun; c.1550–c.1298 B.C.), there was a cat god: none other than Ra. We now know that, according to the Egyptians, power was enclosed in the "ineffable effable, effanineffable" name of the god, as recounted by Frank Henry Brooksbank ("The Story of Ra and Isis," in *Legends of Ancient Egypt*, first published in 1923):

> Now when Ra, the greatest of the gods was created, his father had given him a secret name, so awful that no man dared to seek for it, and so pregnant with power that all the other gods desired to know and possess it too.

Thus, it is no trifling matter that the *Book of the Dead* should refer to the name of the cat Ra, Mau:

> I am the Cat which fought near the Persea Tree in Anu on the night when the foes of Neb-er-tcher were destroyed.
> Who is this Cat?
> This male Cat is Ra himself, and he was called "Mau" because of the speech of the god Sa, who said concerning him: 'He is like (mau) unto that which he hath made'; therefore, did the name of Ra become "Mau."
> (Papyrus of Nebseni, Brit. Mus. No. 9900, Sheet 14, ll. 16ff.)

That the word "mau" more prosaically became a common Egyptian term for cat, akin to our "kitty cat" (hence the name of one of the oldest known feline breeds, the Egyptian Mau) is another story.

The fact remains that, from pyramids to skyscrapers, the issue of "naming the cat" has never ceased to trouble the most sophisticated poets, artists, writers, musicians, actors and directors, with an array of results that this book exhaustively explores (albeit not *every* Tom, Puss, Kitty, Micino, Pallina, Minette and Minouche…).

Indeed, even when a cat is simply called "Cat," there's a reason.

We can start with the motivations cited by Pierre Loti, who, in a letter to his friend Paul Mégnin detailing a list of his felines, commented:

> First. *The Cat* [Le Chat]. He does not have a name. He is the Cat par excellence and we call him 'the Cat,' just as the Romans would say 'Urbs' instead of Rome, the quintessential City.

And then we find the words Truman Capote put in Holly Golightly's mouth in *Breakfast at Tiffany's*:

> "Poor slob," she said, tickling his head, "poor slob without a name. It's a little inconvenient, his not having a name. But I haven't any right to give him one: he'll have to wait until he belongs to somebody. We just sort of took up by the river one day, we don't belong to each other: he's an independent, and so am I."

There are also paradoxical cases, like the cat the singer Norma Tanega named "Dog," perhaps because she walked him around the neighborhood every day (as noted in her debut single "Walkin' My Cat Named Dog"). Then there is the dauntless feline that saved Mrs. Frances Martin from an attacker who entered her bedroom, chasing him away with dreadful scratches: That cat was incongruously named "Mouse."

But there are also those who simply don't care about names, such as the apprentice witch Ms. Price (Angela Lansbury) in the film *Bedknobs and Broomsticks* (1971) who remarked, regarding her black familiar:

> "What do you call your cat?"
> "I don't believe in giving animals ridiculous names. I call him Cosmic Creepers, because that's the name he came with."

In general, however, feline nomenclature is a matter that engaged the likes of men from Cardinal Richelieu to Ernest Hemingway, as well as the pioneer of wireless telegraphy Sir Oliver Lodge, to name just a few of the most passionate ailurophiles (from *ailuros*, Greek for cat).

The thoughts of Englishman Robert Southey (who prose was admired even by his harshest critic Lord Byron) would alone suffice to fill the pages of *Alphacat* if one were to include the "cat-a-log" of cat names he compiled in his "Memoir of the Cats of Greta Hall": Beelzebub of Bath, Senhor Thomas de Lisboa, Lord Nelson, Bona Marietta, William Rufus, Danayr le Roux, Bona Fidelia, Madame Catalani, Madame Bianchi, Pulcheria, Ovid, Virgil, Othello, Zombi, Prester John (then Pope Joan), Rumpelstilzchen and Hurlyburlybuss. None of these names were random, as we can clearly glean from Southey's explanation about the umpteenth black cat he adopted:

> [A]t the unanimous desire of the children, I took upon myself the charge of providing

him with a name, for it is not proper that a cat should remain without one. Taking into consideration his complexion, as well as his sex, my first thought was to call him Henrique Diaz ... but it presently occurred to me that the Zombi [after Zumbi dos Palmares, the last head of the Quilombos] would be an appellation equally appropriate and more dignified. The Zombi, therefore, he was named.

And what can we say about Hemingway's menagerie of more than 50 cats, nearly boasting six toes per paw (in fact, felines with this congenital physical anomaly, known as polydactyl cats, are also referred to as "Hemingway's cats")? They included Ambrose, named after the poet Ambrose Bierce, Bates, Big Boy Peterson, Blindie, Dillinger (later Boise), Ecstasy, Furhouse, Good Will, Pelusa, Princessa, Shopsky (originally Shakespeare and Barbershop), Spendy, Thuster and Willy.

As is the case with humans as well, cats sometimes come up short in the name department. In a letter to the *St. Nicholas Magazine*, Mark Twain wrote:

> There is nothing of continental or inter-national interest to communicate about those cats.
> They had no history; they did not distinguish themselves in any way.
> They died early—on account of being overweighted with their names, it was thought.
> Sour Mash, Appollinaris, Zoroaster, and Blatherskite, – names given them not in an unfriendly spirit, but merely to practice the children in large and difficult styles of pronunciation.
> It was a very happy idea. I mean, for the children.

In any case, the sources of inspiration couldn't be more varied. Catulle Mendès, husband of Judith Gautier, who shared her father's passion for felines, pronounced,

> I had a cat that was named for one of the Valkyries. Mime was as beautiful as love.

In turn, the Comte de Marcellus recalled:

> In Naples I met the cat of the archbishop of Taranto, named Pantalone after a Venetian mask.

And it is difficult not to notice the Shakespearean origin of two of the monsignor's other cats: Desdemona and Otello.

Not all names are quite so scholarly, however. The Siamese cat Poo Jones, the inseparable companion of Vivien Leigh in the 1960s and with her until the actress's death, was named after a young fan, Jones Harris. Jones (Poo, not Harris) would sleep on the actress's shoulders and patiently wait for her in the dressing room until the end of a play—just like Harris.

In some cases, cats have even changed names, such as happened with Victor Hugo's "Gavroche," who became "Chanoine" in reference to his indolence, which resembled that of church canons. However, a further, false etymology is suggested in one of the letters of Hugo's *Le Rhin*, when, as an elderly soldier serving as a guide in a church illustrated the choir stalls, he solemnly declared,

> This is the place of the Chamoines.

Hugo's riposte:

> Don't you think it should be written as *chats-moines* [cat monks]?

A new name often indicates some kind of promotion, as in the case of Bentham's cat, which went from Sir to Reverend Doctor, and of Théophile Gautier's Cuban kitten:

> Its immaculate whiteness caused it to be named Pierrot, and this appellation, when it grew up, developed into Don Pierrot of Navarre, which was infinitely more majestic and smacked of a grandee of Spain.

And this is also the case of the alpha cat in the home of Doris Lessing.

> The other cat, the older brother, has a full ceremonial name, bestowed when he left kittenhood and his qualities had become evident. We called him General Pinknose the Third, paying tribute and perhaps reminding ourselves that even the best looked after cat is going to leave you… Like some people, he acquires new names as time makes its revelations, and recently, because of his moral force and his ability to impose silent judgements on a scene, he became for a time a Bishop, and was known as Bishop Butchkin… He is a magnificent cat…. El Magnifico, the name that suits him best.

But it happens that a name change also corresponds to an unexpected change in… "gender": "Lucinda" becomes "Lucius" and "Olly" becomes "Olivia," but the "Elvis" at the Lennon home kept its name, even after *she* had a litter of kittens!

In any case, even if the name does not have scholarly origins, it must fit like a glove, as asserted in the poem by Thomas Hood, "Choosing their Names".

> Our old cat has kittens three—
> What do you think their names should be?
>
> One is tabby with emerald eyes
> And a tail that's long and slender
> And into a temper she quickly flies
> If you ever by chance offend her.

I think we shall call her this—
I think we shall call her that—
Now, don't you think that Pepperpot
Is a nice name for a cat?

In short, finding the right name requires a certain amount of creativity! For example, while Carl Van Vechten did not devote his encyclopedic erudition on the "tigers in the house" to analyzing their names, he summarized the problem thus:

Naming cats is beyond the powers of the ordinary brain.

This truth is corroborated by the disheartened admission of Samuel Butler:

They say the test of this [literary power] is whether a man can write an inscription. I say, 'Can he name a kitten?' And by this test I am condemned, for I cannot.

In fact, it seems that of the ten names Butler suggested for registration with the Cat Fanciers' Federation, nine were rejected because they had already been used… But, should it prove any consolation, he was in excellent company. In *Lives of Two Cats* (1900), Pierre Loti—yes, the one who named his feline "Cat"—was forced to admit the following with regard to the leading characters in his story, Moumoutte Blanche (Pussy White), the aristocrat, and Moumoutte Grise (Pussy Gray), the kitty from the Chinese slums:

May I be forgiven for having named them both 'Pussy.' To start, I have never had the imagination to name my cats…

Van Vechten, in *The Tiger in the House* (1920) concluded,

The lack of imagination or invention most people display in christening pussies is almost beyond credence.

So perhaps this repertory can offer a few suggestions!

Abélard, a red tabby Persian that belonged to **Avery Hopwood** (1882–1928), accompanied the American playwright on car journeys, sleeping soundly in the passenger seat.

Alphonse, the rain cat featured in *La patte du chat* (1944), a story from the *Les contes du chat perché* (1934–46) by the French writer **Marcel Aymé** (1902–67).

Anubis, the courageous Egyptian cat adopted by archaeologist and amateur detective **Amelia Peabody** and her Egyptologist husband **Radcliffe Emerson** in *The Snake, the Crocodile, and the Dog* (1992), the seventh novel in Elizabeth Peters' saga set in Victorian Egypt. With **Bastet**, Anubis fathered a large brood that would accompany the Emersons on their adventures, to the consternation of the family's loyal but superstitious *reis*, Abdullah: "[Bastet] is not an ordinary cat, as we all know; does not she speak with the young master [Ramses], and heed his commands? This one is a servant of evil, as the cat Bastet is a servant of good. Its very name is a bad omen; was not Anubis the god of cemeteries?"

Atossa, nicknamed "Toss," was the cat of the English poet and literary critic **Matthew Arnold** (1822–88). She is noted to have shown affection only for the first five minutes after waking up in the morning, and she is referred to as "Great Atossa" in Arnold's poem on his dead canary *Poor Matthias* (1882):
"Cruel, but composed and bland,
Dumb, inscrutable and grand,
So Tiberius might have sat
Had Tiberius been a cat."

Ayatollah, the black-and-white cat who makes a brief but beguiling appearance in the French thriller *Diva* (1981), Jean-Jacques Beineix's screen adaptation of the eponymous novel by Daniel Odier (published under the pseudonym Delacorta).

Adorno, Theodor W., the tabby of Argentinean writer **Julio Cortázar** (1914–84), who emigrated to France. Adorno was so named in honor of the German philosopher.

All Ball, the Manx cat chosen as a pet by the "talking" gorilla **Koko** (b. 1971). Dr. Francine Patterson, a communications researcher and Koko's trainer, relayed their touching story in *Koko's Kitten* (1985). He was followed by two other Manxes: Smokey and Lipstick.

Apollinaris, one of the cats of **Mark Twain** (1835–1910), the American author and humorist. It was the feline's silent company— and that of his "colleagues" **Bambino, Blatherskite, Sour Mash** and **Zoroaster**—that led Twain to muse, "If animals could speak, the dog would be a blundering outspoken fellow, but the cat would have the rare grace of never saying a word too much."

Ariel, a red Persian with singular aquatic habits that belonged to **Carl Van Vechten** (1880–1964), the American writer and photographer whose numerous publications on cats included *The Tiger in the House* (1920). "[My] Ariel had no aversion to water; indeed … was accustomed to leap voluntarily into my warm morning tub and she particularly liked to sit in the wash-hand-bowl under the open faucet."
See also Feathers and Scheherazade

Augustus, the late, much-loved cat of **Sir Vidiadhar Surajprasad ("V. S.") Naipaul**, TC (b. 1932), the Trinidad-born British writer who won the Nobel Prize in Literature (2001).

Azrael, the sorcerer **Gargamel**'s red cat who loves to snaffle Smurfs, was created by the Belgian comic artist (1928–92) **Peyo** in the 1960s. "Azrael" is also the name of the angel of death in several religious traditions.

Agata and **Arturo**, the two cats of the Italian novelist **Elsa Morante** (1912–85), which she would sometimes "lend" to theater and film director **Luchino Visconti** (1906–76).
See also Giuseppe

Am, Si's Siamese twin in *Lady and the Tramp*, the animated film produced by Walt Disney in 1955.

Amber, *see Jake*

Arlene, Garfield's "pink" girlfriend in the titular comic strip created by **Jim Davis** (first published in 1978).
See also Nermal

Armando
see New Boy

Asparagus, or **Gus**, the Theatre Cat in **T. S. Eliot**'s *Old Possum's Book of Practical Cats* (1939).
"Gus is the Cat at the Theatre Door.
His name, as I ought to have told you before,
Is really Asparagus.
That's such a fuss
To pronounce, that we usually call him just Gus."
See also Jellylorum, Victoria and Wiscus

for *Turkish Angora*

Originating from Turkey's capital, Ankara (historically, Angora), the breed was one of the most highly regarded in Europe from the eighteenth century. Supplanted by Persians, it nearly became extinct, but the breed was re-established in the 1950s.

Coat: medium-long and silky, no undercoat; the white variety has been certified since 1970, other colors since 1978

Temperament: very affectionate, intelligent and talkative

Ambar and the others ❦

Having seen here a most beautiful breed of cats, which, to be specific, are native to the province of Chorasàn, but of another grace line and another quality than the tabbies that we also cherish … I decided to bring the breed to Rome. In size and shape, they are ordinary cats: their beauty lies in their color, their fur. They are a monkish grey, not striped nor spotted, but the same all over their body … Moreover, their fur is thin, extremely fine, lustrous, and as soft as silk … Their most beautiful aspect is their tail, which is quite large and covered with such long hair that it expands in width by a good half a palm, with an effect like that of squirrels. And, like Squirrels, they curl it over their back, raised like a plume, which is quite charming. They are extremely domestic and, in fact, sometimes Mrs. Maani has no choice but to let some of them in her bed, even between the sheets. I have put together four pairs of males and females … Seeing that I esteem them, my father-in-law, who is good humored, takes great care of them. Every morning, he has them fed tripe in front of him. Sometimes, he enjoys personally cutting up the parts for them and making them jump up to get them; he strokes them and calls them by name—Ambar, Caplàn, Farfanicchio, Ninfa and the others, each with their own. They know him, mew around him, [and] jump on him, which is most enjoyable. I only hope he will not ruin them for me by feeding them too much meat.

PIETRO DELLA VALLE, Letter 9 from Sphahan [Isfahan], in *Viaggi di Pietro della Valle il pellegrino: descritti da lui medesimo in lettere familiari all'erudito suo amico Mario Schipano. La Persia. Parte seconda* [*The Travels of Pietro della Valle, the Pilgrim: Described in Private Letters to the Scholar and his Friend Mario Schipano. Persia, Part Two*], Rome, 1658.

❦The first Turkish Angoras imported to Europe by the Italian traveler Pietro della Valle (1586–1652).

Babou, the pet ocelot (a wild cat; also known as a "dwarf leopard") of the Surrealist artist **Salvador Dalí** (1904–89).

Beauty, the white female cat and main character of *Heartaches of an English Cat* (1842) by Honoré de Balzac (1799-1850): naive and beautiful, she is the neglected wife of the superb Angora, **Puff**—and easy prey of the French charmer, **Brisquet** (*see* p. 18).

Begemot (Behemoth), an enormous black cat who walks on two legs and speaks, is a member of **Woland**'s retinue in **Mikhail Bulgakov**'s *The Master and Margarita* (1967). He also has a penchant for chess, vodka and pistols.

Beppo, the white cat of **Jorge Luis Borges** (1899–1986), Argentinean poet and writer.

Bérénice and **Boudolha**, *see Elsa*

Berlioz, Duchess' black kitten who loves the piano and boxing in *The Aristocats*, a Walt Disney animated feature (1970).
See also Thomas O'Malley

Brilliant, the magnificent white Turkish Angora of **Louis XV**, king of France, is depicted with his master in several portraits.

Buchanan, the black-and-white cat of the English poet and critic **Sir Edmund William Gosse** (1849–1928), and successor of Caruso. "Buchanan was an important member of the household, and had adopted Gosse a year or two before. Though a stray, he was a proud cat, and would never consent to come up to tea unless called or carried by his master in person." (From a description by Sir Osbert Sitwell.)
See also Caruso

Barre-de-Rouille, the "rust" red tabby of the French writer **Joris-Karl Huysmans** (1848–1907) that was also a character in his novel *En ménage* (1881). "It was red, with orange tiger stripes. For that matter, it was a stray cat, but of the large kind. It was huge."

Bébert, the faithful tabby of **Louis-Ferdinand Céline** (Louis Ferdinand Auguste Destouches, 1894–1961), the French writer, critic and physician. Adopted in 1935 by the actor **Robert Le Vigan**, then given to the ballet dancer **Tinou**, in 1942 Bébert chose the house of Céline and his wife Lucette as his, and, for the next ten years, also shared their vicissitudes, including their flight from France as collaborationists of Nazi Germany, described in the Céline's trilogy *Castle to Castle, North* and *Rigadoon* (1957, 1960, 1961). Bébert's life is documented in the 1976 book *Bébert: Le chat de Louis-Ferdinand Céline* by Frédéric Vitoux.

Belaud (1), the grey tabby of **Joachim du Bellay** (1522–60), the French poet and writer, who, in 1558, commemorated his cat in a moving epitaph, which includes the following passage: "Belaud, my great cat is dead. My Belaud, who could be said To be nature's masterpiece Made in the world of cats. Belaud, lethal foe of rats. Belaud, with such beauty worthy of immortality."

Mr. Bigglesworth, **Dr. Evil**'s bald cat in the movie *Austin Powers: International Man of Mystery* (1997). "When Dr. Evil gets angry, Mr. Bigglesworth gets upset. And, when Mr. Bigglesworth gets upset, people DIE."
See also Ted NudeGent

Bismarck
see Disraeli

Butch, one of the many cats of the German-born American poet and author **Charles Bukowski** (1920–94), and mentioned in his autobiographical novel *Women* (1978). In a later interview (2000), Bukowski's wife Linda reflected, "Who were Bukowski's friends? His cats."

Bastet was an ancient Egyptian cat goddess. So what better name for the cat of **Ramses**, Amelia and Radcliffe Emerson's son?
See also Anubis

Beerbohm, named after Herbert Beerbohm Tree, the actor and manager of Her Majesty's Theatre, London. The cat Beerbohm honorably performed for over 20 years, until 1995, as "mouse killer" at the Globe Theatre in London's West End.

Belaud (2), one of the cats of **Pierre Loti** (Julien Viaud, 1850–1923), French writer and naval officer, so called in honor of Joachim du Bellay's cat. "Belaud. Young, stray male… Surges of melancholy, during which he comes to tell me things, with a weak, whining voice."
See also Le Chat and Ratonne

Bettleheim, the cat who talks to **Dr. Dolittle** in the 1998 remake starring Eddie Murphy.

Bimbo, the snowy white, long-haired cat of the Swiss-born painter **Paul Klee** (1879–1940).
See also Fripouille

Boise, dear friend of the American writer and Nobel Laureate **Ernest Hemingway** (1899–1961). Also called "Brother", this black-and-white Cuban cat was Hemingway's regular walking companion, slept in his bed, ate with him and considered himself human, despising the company of other cats. In *Islands in the Stream* (1970), more than 35 pages are dedicated to Boise.
See also Izzy the Cat, Uncle Wolfe and Sir Winston Churchill

for *Bengal*

Recognized as a breed by the International Cat Association in 1986, the Bengal was developed by crossing a domestic cat with an Asian leopard cat as part of research into feline leukemia.

Coat: short and extremely smooth, with rosettes, large spots or horizontal stripes

Temperament: affectionate and not very aggressive; Bengals love to run and jump

Brisquet🐾

Then—but without seeming to look at him—I noticed this fascinating French pussycat: he was unkempt, small, bold and looked nothing like an English cat. His impertinent air, along with the way he wiggled his ears, announced that he was a fun and carefree sort. I must confess that I was tired of the solemnity of English cats and their purely formal distinction. More than anything else, it was their affectation of respectability that seemed ridiculous to me. The excessive nonchalance of this disheveled cat surprised me because it contrasted so violently with everything I saw in London. After all, my life was so absolutely regulated that I knew what I had to do for the remainder of my days, that I was open to all the surprises the French cat's appearance portended … Nevertheless … I feigned that I hadn't heard the declaration and showed apparent indifference, which petrified Brisquet. He stood there, still more astonished because he thought he was quite handsome. I later discovered that he seduced all female cats of good will.

HONORÉ DE BALZAC, "Peines de cœur d'une chatte anglaise"
("Heartaches of an English Cat"), in *Scènes de la vie privée et publique des animaux*
(*Public and private life of animals*), Paris: Flammarion, 1985.

🐾The unscrupulous French seducer responsible for the
heartaches of the English cat, Beauty.

Calvin, a Maltese cat and lover of good literature who showed up one day on the doorstep of **Harriet Beecher Stowe** (1811–96), author of *Uncle Tom's Cabin*. When Stowe left for Florida, Calvin moved to the study of another American writer, **Charles Dudley Warner** (1829–1900), who later celebrated the feline in "Calvin (A Study of Character)," one of a series of essays in *My Summer in a Garden* (1870). "[He] is a reasonable cat, and understands pretty much everything except the binomial theorem."

Carlangas, the cat of the American folk singer and songwriter Joan Baez (b. 1941).

CC (CopyCat), the first cloned domestic cat, a brown-and-white tabby born on December 22, 2001, in Texas.

Charmian, supposedly the name of Cleopatra's cat—and perhaps, therefore, the inspiration for her makeup style.

"Church" (Winston Churchill), the gray cat resurrected in the horror novel *Pet Sematary* (1983) by American author and screenwriter **Stephen King** (b. 1947). The book was made into a movie in 1989, in which it took seven cats to interpret this fictional feline character.
Clovis, **King**'s big tabby that also inspired the name of one of the leading characters in the 1992 horror film *The Sleepwalkers*, for which King wrote the screenplay.

Cobby, the cat of the English poet and novelist Thomas Hardy (1840–1928). Following his death, his ashes were interred in Poets' Corner at Westminster Abbey and his heart buried separately in his birthplace, Stinsford, Dorset. However, Hardy's heart was rumored to have mysteriously disappeared post mortem—and so had Cobby!

Caruso, the beloved black cat—despite his terrible temperament—of the English critic **Sir Edmund William Gosse** (1849–1928). "Caruso, without any question the most ungenerous cat in Christendom. There is no doubt that he is a German at heart, and he rules us on the system of 'frightfulness'. There is a theory that the atrocious soul of Nietzsche has entered into him".
See also Buchanan

Castlerosse, *see The Girl*

Cat, the companion of Holly Golightly (Audrey Hepburn) in *Breakfast at Tiffany's*, Blake Edwards's 1961 film based on the novella by Truman Capote (1958).
See also Orangey

Charles, one of the cats of the Nobel Laureate in Literature Doris Lessing (b. 1919). "One is called Charles, originally Prince Charlie, not after the present holder of that title, but after earlier romantic princes, for he is a dashing and handsome tabby who knows how to present himself. About his character, the less said the better …."
See also El Magnifico, Rufus and p. 78

Chico, the orange tabby belonging to the next-door neighbor of Pope Emeritus Benedict XVI (then, Cardinal Ratzinger).

Ciccio, a big black cat who has officially lived in the Vatican Gardens since 2012.

Cigarette, the cat owned by the French philosopher, Nobel Prize-winning writer and lifelong smoker **Albert Camus** (1913–60). According to **Henri** the existential cat, Camus "stole most of his ideas on absurdism" from Cigarette.

Columbine, the cat of the Scottish writer **Thomas Carlyle** (1795–1881), which got along marvelously with Nero, Mrs. Carlyle's dog—in contrast to the rapport between husband and wife…

Carbonel, the magic black cat who stars in the *Carbonel* series of novels for children created by British author Barbara Sleigh (1906–1982) in 1955 with the first book, *Carbonel: the King of Cats*.

The Cat in the Hat, invented by Dr. Seuss (Theodor Seuss Geisel), first appeared in 1957, when the author accepted a challenge to write an illustrated children's book that contained just 225 words and would not be boring. It was made into a film in 2003.

Childebrand and **Cléopatre**, two of the nine cats of Théophile Gautier (1811–72), the French poet, novelist and critic. "Childebrand was a splendid gutter-cat … 'Cats are the tigers of poor devils,' I once wrote.")
See also Enjolras, Éponine (p.30), Madame-Théophile (62), Zizi (1)

Cleopatra, another masterly interpretation performed by the red tabby **Orangey** (listed as "Rhubarb" in the credits) in *The Comedy of Terrors* (1964), also starring Vincent Price, Peter Lorre and Boris Karloff.

Coquette, *see Gaspard*

Crookshanks, the half-cat, half-kneazle (a magical, cat-like creature with a lion's tale) of **Hermione Granger** in the *Harry Potter* series by J. K. Rowling. In the film version of *Harry Potter and the Prisoner of Azkaban* (2004), Crookshanks was played by two red Persians, **Crackerjack** and **Pumpkin**.
See also Domino

Catarina, the tortoiseshell cat of American poet and novelist **Edgar Allan Poe** (1809–49). The author of the troubling short story *The Black Cat* (1843) was actually quite attached to his own cat, which would often curl up on his shoulders and warmed Poe's ill young wife to the end of her days.
See also Pluton

Chloe and **Crevette**, *see Octavius*

Chopin, the cat of the American writer F. Scott Fitzgerald (1896–1940).

Curly, the first of the LaPerm breed of cat, was born bald at the farm of **Linda** and **Richard Koehl** in Oregon in 1982, but she soon developed a full coat of conspicuously curly hair.

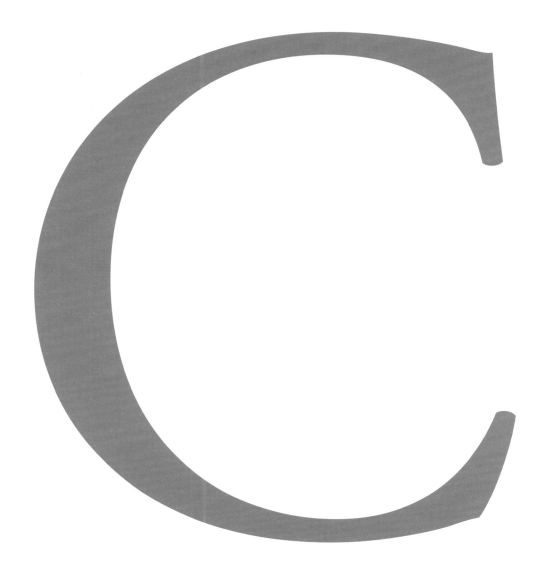

for *Chartreux*

Originally from Turkey, Iran and Syria, this breed may owe its name to French Carthusian monks, who got it from the Templars returning from the Holy Land, and valued its skill at hunting mice, thus protecting food supplies and manuscripts alike.

Coat: dense and velvety, bluish gray
Temperament: peaceful, loyal and quiet

Catzilla ❖

Maury, the Cat Care Society Owner: Morning, gentlemen. I'm Maury. Anything I can help you with?

Lars Smuntz: Ah, hello, Maury. We need a cat.

Maury: Find the one you want and I'll spay or neuter it myself!

Lars: Well, these are all kittens. We were hoping for an older cat, one with experience.

Maury: That's a switch. Most people like the cute little ones. Experience with what?

Ernie Smuntz: Mouse hunting.

Maury: Oh, all cats are good mousers.

Ernie: Yes, but you see, we have huge rats, the size of sumo wrestlers, and lots of 'em, so we really need a ferocious feline, preferably one with a history of mental illness. I'm talkin' one mean pussy.

Lars: Yeah! A vicious cat, difficult to love. You got any of those knocking around your cages?

Maury: Funny you should ask. I had given up hope of anyone wanting him. We were about to gas him again.

Lars, Ernie: "Again"?

Maury: He's spent most of his whole life in that box, I expect.

[*zoom into the label on the cage*]

Ernie: "Catzilla"?

Maury: The guys who clean up call him that. But you can call him anything you want. I'd say he looks like a "Fluffy."

Lee Evans (Lars), Nathan Lane (Ernie) and Ervnie Sabella (Maury) in
MouseHunt, movie, directed by Gore Verbinski, USA: DreamWorks Studios, 1997.

❖In the movie *MouseHunt*, the psychopathic cat hired by
the Smuntz brothers in the (vain) attempt to get rid of the
small but destructive "lodger" in the family mansion.

Dandelion, the kleptomaniac cat of **Sara Peacock**, from Spotwood, New Zealand, who discovered that her cat was responsible for a spate of local burglaries. Over the course of two years, Dandelion stole more than 700 items from their neighbors, displaying a particular penchant for socks

Dabado, *see Waif*

Delilah, the tortoiseshell cat that Queen's lead vocalist **Freddie Mercury** (1946-1991) referred to as "the apple of my eye." She is celebrated in the album *Innuendo*. "You make me so very happy / When you cuddle up and go to sleep beside me. / And then you make me slightly mad / When you pee all over my Chippendale suite." *See also Jerry*

Dick and **Dora**, the cats of the English novelist **Frances Hodgson Burnett** (1849–1924). Dora, snuggled in her arms, encouraged the literary attempts of the author—who would became famous for children's books such as *Little Lord Fauntleroy* (1886)—when, at the age of just 15, Burnett started to submit stories to magazines. Dick participated in New York's first cat show.

Dinah, the cat of **Alice Liddell** (1852–1934), who inspired **Lewis Carroll**'s stories. The cat would also become a literary character in the sequel of *Alice's Adventures in Wonderland* (1865), *Through the Looking Glass* (1871), as the mother of the white kitten **Snowdrop** and the black one named **Kitty**. "The way Dinah washed her children's faces was this: first she held the poor thing down by its ear with one paw, and then with the other paw she rubbed its face all over, the wrong way, beginning at the nose: and just now, as I said, she was hard at work on the white kitten, which was lying quite still and trying to purr—no doubt feeling that it was all meant for its good." *See also the Cheshire Cat, p. 46*

Dog, the name that singer **Norma Tanega** (b. 1939) gave to her cat, which she would take out for walks, a ritual about which she sang in her 1966 hit *Walkin' My Cat Named Dog*.

Domino, the feline companion—along with Bubbles—of actress **Emma Watson** (b. 1990), who played Hermione Granger in the *Harry Potter* film series. *See also Croockshanks*

Doyenne, the cat of the Swiss philosopher **Jean-Jacques Rousseau** (1712–78).

Dandelo (also "Dandilo"), the unfortunate cat in the 1958 version of *The Fly*, on which David Cronenberg's 1986 remake was based.

Desdemona, one of the cats of **Giuseppe Capecelatro** (1744–1836), archbishop of Taranto and an Italian statesman, described by the Irish novelist Lady Morgan. "Between the first and the second course, the door opened, and several enormously large and beautiful cats were introduced, by the names of Pantalone, Desdemona, Otello, and other dramatic cognomina. They took their places on chairs near the table, and were as silent, as quiet, as motionless, and as well behaved, as the most bon ton table in London could require. On the Bishop requesting one of the chaplains to help the signora Desdemona to something, the butler step up to his Lordship and observed, 'Desdemona will prefer waiting for the roast'."

Didi, one of the cats of the French-Polish scientist Marie Curie (1867–1934), who was awarded the Nobel Prize in Physics (1903) and Chemistry (1911).

Dino, the cat living a double life: by day, the companion of a little girl named **Zoe**, and, by night, the assistant of the thief **Nico**, scrambling across Parisian rooftops, in the French animated film *A Cat in Paris* (2012).

Disraeli, one of the cats of **Florence Nightingale** (1820–1910), the British nurse and pioneer of modern healthcare. Nightingale named each of her 60 cats after a politician. She also had a Gladstone and a large Persian by the name of **Bismarck**.

Duchess, the lead character in *The Aristocats*, the Walt Disney animated film released in 1970. She is mother to **Toulouse**, **Marie** and **Berlioz**. *See also Thomas O'Malley*

Damn Cat (also "D.C."), alternative names for **Pancho**, the fictional cat created by **Gordon** and **Mildred Gordon** in their novel *Undercover Cat* (1963), in which he helps to solves the case of a bank robbery. The story inspired the Disney movie *That Darn Cat* (1965), in which D.C. is played by a Siamese cat called **Syn**, as well as its 1997 remake with Christina Ricci.

Desdémonette (also **Démonette**), the black cat, "Princess of Mauritania," of the French poet, novelist and critic **Jules Amédée Barbey d'Aurevilly** (1808–89). She was the subject of numerous letters the writer exchanged with Miss Louise Read, who took care of her in his absence. In 1884, Barbey d'Aurevilly wrote: "One might say that the main interest in your life is to send me news about the cat!"

Miss DiPesto, born in Montana in 1987, is the stray foundation cat of the Selkirk Rex breed, the curly-haired felines that arose as a result of a random genetic mutation. She was named as a tribute to the curly coif of the secretary in the television series *Moonlighting*.

Dom Gris, *see Grisette*

Don Tarquinio, the distinguished Persian in "The Reticence of Lady Anne", a short story by **Saki** (H. H. Munro, 1870–1916) published in *Reginald in Russia and Other Sketches* (1910). "His pedigree was as flawlessly Persian as the rug … The page-boy, who had Renaissance tendencies, had christened him Don Tarquinio. Left to themselves, Egbert and Lady Anne would unfailingly have called him Fluff, but they were not obstinate."

for *Devon Rex*

The first Devon Rex, distinguished by its intriguing curly fur, was discovered in the English county of Devon in 1960. Initially mistaken for the Cornish Rex, it was recognized as a separate breed in 1967.

Coat: short, curly and slightly coarse; shedding less noticeable than in other breeds

Temperament: affectionate and intelligent, very curious and sociable

Dewey Readmore Books*

1. If you are feeling particularly lonely and want more attention from the staff, sit on whatever papers, project or computer they happen to be working on—but do so with your back to the person, and act aloof, so as not to appear too needy. Also, continually rub against the leg of the staff person who is wearing dark brown, blue or black clothes, for maximum effect.

...

5. Your humans must realize that all boxes that enter the library are yours. It doesn't matter how large, how small, how full the box is—it is yours! If you cannot fit your entire body into the box, then use whatever part of your body fits, to assume ownership for naptime. (I have used one or two paws, my head, or even just my tail to gain entry, and each works equally well for a truly restful sleep.)

Vikki Myron, "Dewey's Guide for Library Cats," in Sandra Choron, Harry Choron and Arden Moore, *Planet Cat. A Cat-alog*, Boston: Houghton Mifflin, 2007, pp. 155–156.

*The Maine Coon that lived at the Spencer Public Library, Iowa, from 1988 until 2006. Abandoned in the book return drop, he was officially adopted by the library staff, with specific institutional duties drawn up with the help of the library director, Vikki Myron.

Ebène, one of the three cats of French philosopher and historian **Hippolyte Adolphe Taine** (1828–93). To Ebène, Mitonne and Puss, "their friend, master and servant" dedicated 12 sonnets, published posthumously—and without Taine's family's consent—in a literary supplement of the French newspaper *Le Figaro*.
"O my happy cats! Your peaceful purring the voice of that invisible heart reaches the secret of the mystical universe." (from Sonnet XII, "The Absolute," 1883).

Edgar, with Herman, the Devon Rex cats of **Dita Von Teese** (b. Heather Renée Sweet, 1972), the American queen of neo-burlesque.

El Brooksha, according to Sephardic Jewish folklore, is the name of a gigantic cat that sucked the blood of newborns and transformed itself into Lilith, Adam's first wife, after he was driven from the Garden of Eden.

El Magnifico (also "General Pinknose the Third," "Bishop Butchkin"), the magnificent black-and-white cat of **Doris Lessing** (b. 1919), who shared the house with the Nobel Laureate along with his brother Charles and the former stray Rufus (p. 78).
"Every evening The General, El Magnifico Butchkin, came to lie by me on the sofa for a while, to establish his right to this position, before going to his favourite place on top of the basket. This place by me was the best place, because Butchkin thought it was: Charles, for instance, was not allowed it."

Elsa, along with Thaïs, Paphnuce, Bérénice and Boudolha, is one of the five cats the French writer **Ernest Léon La Jeunesse** (1874–1917) brought with him from Nancy to Paris, as recounted in his "contemporary novel" *L'Inimitable* (1899).

Elvis, the cat of **John Lennon's mother**. According to the singer's half-sister, Julia Baird, says: "Mummy liked [Elvis Presley] to such an extent that when we got a kitten (at my insistence) it was christened Elvis. The cat later produced a litter of kittens in the bottom of the kitchen cupboard – so we realized our mistake – but the name remained the same!"

Enrique DeLome, *see Valeriano Weyler*

Étoile, the white Angora of **Gustave Courbet** (1819–77), portrayed at the French artist's feet in *The Artist's Studio* (1855) (Musée d'Orsay, Paris).

Enjolras, brother of Gavroche and Éponine (p. 30), the three black cats of **Théophile Gautier** (1811–72), French poet, novelist and critic.
"There was something theatrical and grandiloquent about him, and he seemed to pose like an actor who attracts admiration. His motions were slow, undulating, and full of majesty; he seemed to be always stepping on a table covered with china ornaments and Venetian glass, so circumspectly did he select the place where he put down his foot."
See also Childebrand and Cléopâtre, Madame-Théophile (62), Zizi (1)

Eudora, the library cat of the Cave Spring Public Library, Georgia, since 2003. More than 800 library cats are known of around the world, while current residents (including statues, stuffed animals and ghost cats) total 302.

Eureka (also "Pink Kitten"), **Dorothy**'s stray, first introduced in the book *Dorothy and the Wizard in Oz* by **L. Frank Baum** (1908).

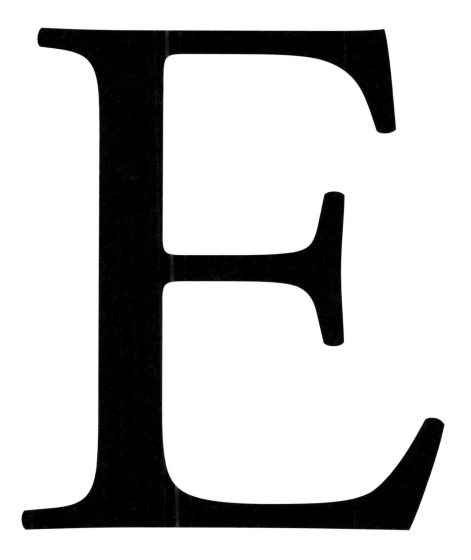

for *European Shorthair*

One of the most widespread cats in the world, it arrived in Europe aboard Phoenician ships sailing from North Africa. Since 1982, only the Scandinavian type bred from short-haired cats can boast the title of European Shorthair.
Coat: short and glossy; lies flat
Temperament: intelligent and active, but varying widely from one to another

Eponine ♣

The cat who bore the name of the interesting Eponine was more lissome and slender in shape than her brothers. Her mien was quite peculiar to herself, owing to her somewhat long face, her eyes slanting slightly in the Chinese fashion, and of a green like that of the eyes of Pallas Athene …. There never was a more sensitive, nervous, and electric animal. If she were stroked two or three times, in the dark, blue sparks came crackling from her fur…. She trots up when she hears the bell ring, welcomes my visitors, leads them into the drawing-room, shows them to a seat, talks to them—yes, I mean it, talks to them—with croonings and cooings and whimpers quite unlike the language cats make use of among themselves, and which simulate the articulate speech of man. You ask me what it is she says? She says, in the plainest possible fashion: "Do not be impatient; look at the pictures or chat with me, if you enjoy that. My master will be down in a minute." And when I come in she discreetly retires to an arm-chair or on top of the piano, and listens to the conversation without breaking in upon it, like a well-bred animal that is used to society. Sweet Eponine has given us so many proofs of intelligence, kindly disposition, and sociability that she has been promoted, by common consent, to the dignity of a *person*, for it is plain that a higher order of reason than instinct guides her actions … So Eponine's chair is placed beside mine at lunch and dinner, and on account of her size she is allowed to rest her fore paws upon the edge of the table.

THÉOPHILE GAUTIER, "My Private Menagerie," in F. C. de Sumichrast (Trans., Ed.), *The Works of Théophile Gautier*, vol. 19, online, Project Gutenberg, 2009 (first published, 1902), 30760.

♣The remarkably civilized Eponine, who, plate after plate—including dessert—shared meals with Gautier, had just one fault: She was apt to refuse to eat soup when she was certain (following a kitchen reconnaissance) that the main dish would be fish. Nevertheless, the threat that she would not be allowed to enjoy the entrée unless she finished her soup first was enough to make her lick the bowl clean…

Feathers, the pianist cat of American writer and photographer **Carl Van Vechten** (1880–1964). "Sometimes she walks sedately from one end of the keyboard to the other, producing an exotic succession of tones; at other times she pounces on a group of keys ... On these occasions she will leap wildly from treble to bass, tearing tone and melody to tatters. ... She has a particular penchant ... for music at night and it is no rarity to awaken at 2 a.m. to hear Feathers attempting prodigious scales."
See also Ariel and Sheherazade

Félimare, one of the 14 cats, with **Gazette, Mimi-Piaillon, Mounard-le-Fougueux, Rubis-sur-l'Ongle, Serpolet,** and **Soumise** taken care of thanks to the extremely generous bequest of **Armand Jean Du Plessis** (1585–1642), cardinal and duke of Richelieu and chief minister to King Louis XIII of France, on his death.
See also, Lucifer, Ludovic-le-Cruel, Ludoviska, Perruque and Racan, Pyrame and Thisbé

Felix the Cat, the first cartoon cat, who appeared on the big screen for Paramount Pictures in the 1920s. In fact, he debuted in 1919 with the name "Master Tom," in a short entitled *Feline Follies*, directed by Otto Messmer

Fiocchino, the cat of the Trieste Astronomical Observatory and one of the many feline companions of the Italian astrophysicist **Margherita Hack** (1922–2013), who dedicated the book *I gatti della mia vita* (2012) to him and to **Ciompa, Cirilla, Checca, Cicino, Celestino, Geppetta** and **Genny.**

Fripouille (also "Fritzi"), the tabby of the Swiss-born painter **Paul Klee** (1879–1940). He may have been the model for the painting *Cat and Bird* (1928), now at the Museum of Modern Art (MoMA) in New York.
See also Bimbo

Fafner and **Fasolt**, cats who dined at the table of **Catulle Mendès** (1841–1909), the French author and poet.

Felis, the cat to whom the English author and theologian **John Jortin** (1698–1770) dedicated a moving epitaph in Latin. In it, Felis implores Proserpine to permit him go home for just one night and let him whisper to his owner that he will be faithful even across the Styx, in the kingdom of the dead.

Felix-Mendelssohn-Bartholdy-Shedlock-Runciman-Felinis, the cat of **John F. Runciman** (1866–1916), music critic for the London-based *Saturday Review*. At the age of six months, he spat at horse-drawn carriages, while, as an adult, he attempted to "play" a viola by dragging its bow across the floor.

Figaro, the "good" cat in Walt Disney's *Pinocchio* (1940).
See also Gideon

Foss, the beloved half-tailed tabby of the English writer, poet and illustrator **Edward Lear** (1812–88). He was the subject of many of Lear's later drawings, including a series of caricatures titled "The Heraldic Blazon of Foss the Cat", subsequently published in *Nonsense Songs and Stories* (1895, 9th ed.). Lear moved to San Remo, Italy, and, when he had his second villa built (because the view from the original one was ruined by a hotel), he asked that it be an exact replica of the first, because otherwise Foss would not approve. Lear died two months after Foss, who was buried in his Italian garden.

Frätzibutzi, one of the cats of the writer **Carmen Sylva** (pseudonym of Elisabeth of Wied, the German-born queen of Romania) (1843–1916). Frätzibutzi is mentioned in an illustrated article by Sylva titled "My Kittens" (*Century Magazine*, August 1908), along with **Vulpi (Füchschen), Lilliput, Püffchen** and **Misikatz (Micki).**

Frontin, the cat of the French novelist and writer **Charles Paul de Kock** (1793–1871), about whom de Kock observes in his memoirs, "Frontin was no cat; in goodness of heart he was a poodle, in sobriety a camel, and in intelligence a monkey."

Félicette, the French "Astrocat" (so baptized by the British press), was the first cat to be sent into space (October 18, 1963)—and survive. The event was commemorated by a stamp, but it bore the name "Félix." In fact, of the ten cats trained by the French government for the space flight (the other eight were rejected because they ate too much), the original "Astrocat" selected was a tabby called **Félix**, but he managed to get away in the nick of time and was replaced by the black-and-white Félicette.

Fletch, one of the cats of the American writer **William S. Burroughs** (1914–97). The author of *Naked Lunch* (1959) celebrated his feline companions in his autobiographical novella *The Cat Inside* (1986), and he devoted his last thought to them in his diary just before he died. "Only thing can resolve conflict is love, like I felt for Fletch and **Ruski, Spooner,** and **Calico.** Pure love. What I feel for my cats present and past. ... Love? What is It? Most natural painkiller what there is. LOVE."

Frimas, *see Neige*

Fritz the Cat, the humanized free-living feline in the underground comics of **Robert Crumb** (b. 1943), first published in 1965, followed by a book in 1969 and a movie in 1972. Fritz was modeled on Crumb's real cat, **Fred**.

Frou-Frou, one of the cats of the English painter **Sir William Nicholson** (1872–1949), who created a series of sketches at Chartwell, Kent, the home of Sir Winston Churchill, one of which—*Study for Breakfast at Chartwell II*—depicts **Tango**, the Churchill family's "marmalade cat."
See also The Girl

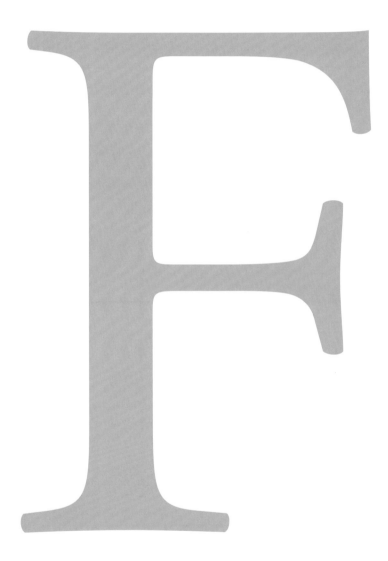

for *Fawn (Abyssinian)*

The Fawn, a variety of Abyssinian named for the color of its fur, is one of the most popular breeds in the United States. It is thought that the Abyssinian was imported to England in the 1860s from what is now Ethiopia (historically, Abyssinia). It was first listed as a breed in 1882.

Coat: short, rosy dove gray

Temperament: intelligent, playful, fearless and friendly

Fanchette ❧

A happy creature, Fanchette has taken her captivity with good grace. Without protest, she has agreed to deposit her little horrors in a receptacle filled with sawdust, dissimulated between the bed and the wall, and—absorbed—I enjoy studying her countenance during the phases of this important operation.

Fanchette washes her hind paws, carefully between her toes. A self-possessed expression that says nothing. Washing stops suddenly: a serious and slightly preoccupied expression. Abrupt change of position; she sits on her rear. Eyes cold and almost severe. She gets up, takes three steps and sits down again. Then, irrevocable decision, a leap from the bed, a dash to the receptacle, digging… and then nothing. The air of indifference reappears. But it doesn't last. Her distraught eyebrows are drawn; she digs through the sawdust again feverishly, scampers over it, looks for the right place and, for three minutes, her gaze fixed and absent, she seems to concentrate hard. Because, quite often, she's constipated. At last, she slowly gets up and meticulously covers up the corpse, with the absorbed air befitting this sort of a funereal operation. Short superfluous scratching around the receptacle and, without pausing an instant, she arches up in a diabolical leap, the prelude to a sabbatic dance, the step of liberation. Then I laugh and shout, "Mélie, come quickly and change the kitty litter!"

WILLY [Colette], *Claudine à Paris* (*Claudine in Paris*), Paris: P. Ollendorff, 1901.

❧The cat who accompanied Claudine to Paris when she moved there from Montigny (the setting for the first novel in the series, *Claudine à l'école* (*Claudine at School*, 1900, which takes the form of a diary). Fanchette was also the name of the one of the cats of Sidonie Gabrielle Colette (1873–1954), author of the *Claudine* series, who published her first books using her husband's pseudonym "Willy" (Henry Gauthier-Villars).

Gavroche (1), *see Enjolras*

Garfield, the fat, lazy, red tabby who is the key character in the eponymous comic strip by **Jim Davis**, first published on June 19, 1978, and today a merchandising empire that includes books, gadgets and movies. He was named after the author's grandfather. One of his many sayings is, "The best things in life are edible."
See also Arlene and Nermal

General Sterling Price, the huge red cat of **Rooster Cogburn** (played by John Wayne) in the popular Western *True Grit* (1969), directed by Henry Hathaway.

Giuseppe, one of the cats of the Italian writer **Elsa Morante** (1912–85). "I believe the greatest thing I was seeking for myself in life was this: friendship. But I've found only one true friendship: that of my cat Giuseppe." (*Letters*)
See also Agata and Arturo

Grimalkin (1) (from "gray" and "malkin," archaic for "cat") is the traditional Scottish name for old female cats associated with magic. It cannot be a coincidence that this was also the name of the cat of "**Nostradamus**," the Latinized name of the French physician, apothecary, astrologist and, above all, reputed seer Michel de Nostredame (1503–66).

Grisette, the cat of **Antoinette du Ligier de la Garde Deshoulières** (1638–94), a French poet and writer of numerous love letters, in verse, between Grisette and other French felines, such as **Tata**, the cat of the Marquise de Montglas, and **Dom Gris**, the cat of the Duchesse de Béthune.

Ginger, the red cat that runs the village shop along with the terrier Pickles in *The Tale of Ginger and Pickles* (originally published as *Ginger and Pickles*) (1909), created by **Beatrix Potter**.

Granpa (formerly "Pierre"), previous holder of the record for "oldest cat ever," awarded by The Guinness Book of World Records, at the advanced age of 34 years, 2 months and 4 hours. (The current record-holder is **Creme Puff**, who lived for 38 years and 3 days—and hailed from the same household as Granpa.) He was a rare hairless Sphynx, lost in Texas by his French owner and adopted in 1970 by a plumber, **Jack Perry**. Despite his age—and thanks, perhaps, to a broccoli-rich diet—this valuable pedigree puss won numerous beauty contests, too.

Grimalkin (2), the cat for whom the then-16-year-old **Christina Rossetti** (1830–94) composed a funerary poem, which included the lines: "Of a noble race she came, / And Grimalkin was her name … And whoever passes by / The poor grave where Puss doth lie, / Softly, softly let him tread, / Nor disturb her narrow bed."

Grumpy Cat, the feline with the world's biggest scowl on her face (although she seems to be good-natured). Because of her constant frown, she became an Internet celebrity just a few months after she was born in 2012. "I had fun once. It was awful."

Gavroche (2), the magnificent Angora of the French poet, playwright and novelist Victor Hugo (1802–85). Also called "Chanoine" as his laziness was reportedly akin to the proverbial idleness of canons, Gavroche established an armed truce with the three white ducks of Hugo's granddaughter Jeanne, although he would promptly chase them as soon as the girl turned her back.

The Girl, the black cat of the British painter **Sir William Nicholson** (1872–1949) and twin sister of Castelrosse, "whose welcoming purr is guaranteed to penetrate stone walls."
See also Frou-Frou

Gazette, *see Félimare*

Gideon, the fox's sidekick in the animated Disney movie *Pinocchio* (1940), which was inspired by Carlo Collodi's children's book *The Adventures of Pinocchio* (*Le avventure di Pinocchio*) (1883), first published as a serial in Italian in 1881.
See also Figaro

The Great Mr. Thomas, the magnificent tabby of the British painter **Philip Wilson Steer** (1860–1942), the latter referred to by his friends as "Old Pussy Steer" because of his love of cats. Mr. Thomas had his own armchair across from Steers, and, if a guest happened to sit in it, the cat would stare at him with "revolted patience until Steer would finally explain, 'I'm afraid you are sitting in Mr. Thomas's chair.'"

Gris-Gris, the black cat lost in *When the Cat's Away* (*Chacun cherche son chat*) (1996), a French film directed by Cédric Klapisch and set entirely in the Parisian quarter of Bastille. There's a happy ending: he's finally found.

Gypsy, one of the four cats of the American art collector **Peggy Guggenheim** (1898–1979).

for *Gatto* ('cat' in Italian)

Also, *gato* (in Spanish) and *gatz* (in Armenian). The *gatto selvatico* (*Felis silvestris*), or wildcat, is the ancestor of the domestic cat and is found all over the world. Its ability to adapt to a wide range of habitats, from savannahs to mountains, is reflected in the diverse physical traits of the species. The European variety resembles the tabby cat, but is more muscular.

Coat: medium-haired, dense, with dark stripes
Temperament: feral…

Gip ❖

It is rather an odd coincidence that in the village inn where I am writing a portion of this book, including the present chapter, there should be three cats, unlike one another in appearance and habits as three animals of different and widely separated species … The last is Gip, a magnificent creature, a third bigger than an average-sized cat – as large and powerfully built as the British wild cat, a tabby with opaline eyes, which show a pale green colour in some lights. These singular eyes, when I first saw this animal, almost startled me with their wild, savage expression; nor was it a mere deceptive appearance, as I soon found. I never looked at this animal without finding these panther or lynx eyes fixed with a fierce intensity on me, and no sooner would I look towards him than he would crouch down, flatten his ears, and continue to watch my every movement as if apprehending a sudden attack on his life. It was many days before he allowed me to come near him without bounding away and vanishing, and not for two or three weeks would he suffer me to put a hand on him.

W. H. HUDSON, *A Shepherd's Life: Impressions of the South Wiltshire Downs*,
London: Methuen & Co. Ltd, 1910, pp. 185–187.

❖ The cat described by the naturalist and ornithologist
William Henry Hudson (1841–1922) in his work on the
English countryside *A Shepherd's Life*. Of gipsy origins and
then adopted by the innkeeper, Gip was a "most inveterate
rat-killer … he cannot destroy fewer than three hundred to
four hundred rats in the year."

Hamilcar, the cat of the French Nobel Laureate for Literature **Anatole France** (Jacques Anatole Thibault) (1844–1924), and the cat featured in his first novel, *The Crime of Sylvestre Bonnard* (1881). While the bibliophile **Bonnard** praises—with growing enthusiasm—the virtues of Hamilcar, who vaunts "the formidable aspect of a Tatar warrior and the slumbrous grace of a woman of the Orient," in turn, Hamilcar thinks this "old-book man … talks to no purpose at all while our housekeeper never utters a word which is not full of good sense, full of significance—containing either the announcement of a meal or the promise of a whipping. One knows what she says. But this old man puts together a lot of sounds signifying nothing."

Hello Kitty, the white cat with a red ribbon created by the designer **Yuko Shimizu** (b. 1946) and launched by the Japanese company Sanrio in 1974. Hello Kitty is today the empress of merchandizing, from undergarments to hairclips.

Hiddigeigei, a black tomcat whose 13 songs feature in the mock-heroic epic poem *The Trumpeter of Säckingen* (1884) by the German poet and novelist **Joseph Victor von Scheffel** (1826–86).

Hodge, one of the cats of **Samuel Johnson** (1709–84), the English critic, lexicographer and writer. According to James Boswell's remarkable biography (1791) of Johnson, he personally purchased oysters for his cosseted cat (to avoid troubling his servants with the task). A bronze statue of Hodge, complete with oyster, features in the courtyard outside 17 Gough Square, London, where he and Dr. Johnson resided together.
See also Lily

Horace, Nick's "illegal" cat in the children's book *Nick and the Glimmung* (1966; first published 1988) by the American sci-fi author **Philip K. Dick** (1928–82).
See also Magnificat

Huan, the Thai cat who, while reputed to be a formidable mouse hunter, adopted a little mouse found in a closet and baptized "Jerry." The two became inseparable, as documented in the Internet video clip *Do Cats Really Love Mice?*

Humphrey, the "Chief Mouser to the Cabinet Office" at 10 Downing Street, London. He was adopted after wandering in as a stray while Margaret Thatcher was prime minister, in 1989, and went on to serve under her, John Major and Tony Blair, before "retiring" six months after the 1997 general election. In March 2006, a Downing Street spokesman announced to the nation that Humphrey had passed away.
See also Wilberforce

Harold, one of the cats of **Horace Walpole** (1717–97), 4th Earl of Orford, a politician, antiquarian and writer. In his letters he mentions another cat, Zara.
See also Selima

Henri (Le Chat Noir), an American black-and-white cat, is the despondent star of a series of Internet shorts by **Will Braden**. Henri, like any French existentialist, is ridden by angst (often brought on by L'imbécile blanc, with whom he shares his Seattle household). "Some have asked if I dream in French or English. It is neither. I dream in false hope."

Hinze, the name used for the cat in the 1797 satirical stage version of *Puss in Boots* by **Ludwig Tieck** (1773–1853). "If we had not, in our intercourse with human beings, acquired a certain contempt for speech we could all speak."

Holly, the New Zealand cat who demonstrates a typically female passion for shoes. The rewards she reaps from her naughty nocturnal expeditions are stowed in boxes behind her home in Manurewa, ready for the booty's original owners to reclaim the footwear this feline's filched.

Hugh, the cat and main inspiration (though black) of the perpetually hungry white cat in the comic strip *Simon's Cat*, by the British animator **Simon Tofield** (b. 1973). Simon's other cats—Teddy, Jess and Maisie—have also contributed to the characterization of his fictional feline.

Hamlet, the first feline guest at New York's luxurious Algonquin Hotel. This stray, taken in by the owner **Frank Case** in the late 1930s, went on to become the hotel's "most famous guest." This role is currently held by a female feline—called Matilda.

Heathcliff, the red cat featured in a comic strip of the same name created by **George Gately** (1928–2001) in 1973, and brought to the screen in 1980. A friend of the cat Riff-Raff, Heathcliff is in love with the white cat Sonja.

Herman, *see Edgar*

Hester, the only cat **Andy Warhol** (1928–87) owned that wasn't named **Sam**, as evidenced by his privately printed book *25 Cats Name [sic] Sam and One Blue Pussy* (1954). It seems that the father of Pop Art and his mother Julia Warhola always had a houseful of cats, and ended up giving countless of them away to friends.

Hope, the name given to a cat who survived the devastation of the 9/11 attacks on the World Trade Center while protecting her three new-born kittens: Freedom, Amber and Flag.

Hugo, the cat who appeared with a very young, nearly naked Madonna (b. 1958) in a photo shoot by Martin H.M. Schreiber (b. 1946) (New York, 1979), from which several images were later published in *Playboy* (1985).

Hurlyburlybuss, one of the many cats of **Robert Southey** (1774–1843), English Romantic poet, prose writer and man of letters. In letters to his daughter, Southey drew up a "cat-a-log" of the many guests staying at Greta Hall, their home in the Lake District, dwelling in particular on the "strong enmity" between Hurlyburlybuss, "master of the green and garden," and Rumpelstilzchen, master of the house.
See also Ovid (p. 70) and Zombi

for *Himalayan*

With the build and coat of a Persian and the coloring and blue eyes of a Siamese, this breed was first recognized (as a long-haired colorpoint) in 1955 by Great Britain's Governing Council of the Cat Fancy (GCCF), and then, in 1957, as a Himalayan by the U.S. Cat Fanciers' Association. Its name was inspired by its body and point color contrast, seen in other colorpoint animals such as the Himalayan rabbit.

Coat: long-haired, very dense, silky
Temperament: playful and talkative

Hinse of Hinsefield*

Among the other important and privileged members of the household who figured in attendance at the dinner was a large gray cat, who, I observed, was regaled from time to time with tit-bits from the table. This sage grimalkin was a favorite of both master and mistress, and slept at night in their room; and Scott laughingly observed that one of the least wise parts of their establishment was that the window was left open at night for puss to go in and out. The cat assumed a kind of ascendancy among the quadrupeds—sitting in state in Scott's arm-chair, and occasionally stationing himself on a chair beside the door, as if to review his subjects as they passed, giving each dog a cuff beside the ears as he went by. This clapper-clawing was always taken in good part; it appeared to be, in fact, a mere act of sovereignty on the part of grimalkin, to remind the others of their vassalage; which they acknowledged by the most perfect acquiescence. A general harmony prevailed between sovereign and subjects, and they would all sleep together in the sunshine.

WASHINGTON IRVING, "Abbotsford and Newstead Abbey," in *The Crayon Miscellany*,
Volume 2, Philadelphia: Carey, Lea & Blanchard, 1835.

*The proud tabby of Sir Walter Scott (1771–1832), the
Scottish novelist and poet, portrayed by the Scottish
portrait painter John Watson Gordon on the writer's desk,
while, at his feet, a safe distance away, is his bloodhound,
capable of confronting a wolf but not the resident feline.
In fact, the harmony between cats and dogs described by
Irving did not always reign supreme: "I heard my friend
set up some most piteous howls (and I assure you the noise
was no joke), all occasioned by his fear of passing Puss, who
had stationed himself on the stairs." (W. Scott, in a letter to
Joanna Baillie, April 12 1816)

Iblis, one of the cats of **Judith Gautier** (also known as **Judith Walter and Judith Mendès**) (1845–1917), the French author, Oriental scholar and eldest daughter of Théophile Gautier, whose passion for cats she shared. Together with Bébé, Crevette and Lilith, Iblis was of great help in the preparation of the Christmas' tree.
See also Satan

L'Infâme (also Charles Scherer),

one of the cats of the French satirist and playwright **Georges Courteline** (Georges Victor Marcel Moineaux) (1858–1929), "the father of all the creatures roaming the hill of Montmartre," as described by his friend Paul Mégnin (author of *Notre ami le chat*, 1899). The latter went on to say: "Courteline's cats are good people and they allowed themselves to be portrayed; but the master rebels against any sort of interview. All I was able to obtain are the names of his feline companions, and what names! They certainly cannot deny they are from Montmartre: the Purotin de la rue Ruisseau; Charles Scherer, alias L'Infâme, alias the Terreur de Clignancourt; the Mère dissipée; the Petit Turbulent; and the Rouquin de Montmartre."

Isis, the mysterious black cat of **Gary Seven** (played by Robert Lansing) in the "Assignment: Earth" episode (1968) in the second season of the original *Star Trek* series. Isis can not only take on a human appearance and communicate telepathically with people, but can also understand their words. This character was actually played by three different cats, including **Sambo**, because, as Lansing recounts: "[In] those days, the theory was that you couldn't train cats. Cats would have a certain propensity: One would like somebody, would want to follow them around, so that day, you would release the cat that would probably do what you wanted it to do."

Isoline, the cat of Dr. **Stephen Artault de Vevey**, a French researcher who investigated, among other topics, the comparative intelligence of humans and other animals, and published an article entitled "Des Actes raisonnés chez le Chat" (1903). It is hard to say how "rational" Isoline's propensity for water was: She loved to bathe by leaping straight into the tub. She also had no problem making herself understood by Dr. Artault's neighbors, who lived on the fifth floor and whom she loved to visit. When meowing wasn't enough to get them to open the door, she would start scratching it and, as a last resort, would even pull the bell cord!

Icarus, cat of the American boxing legend **Muhammad Ali** (b. Cassius Marcellus Clay, Jr., 1942), gold medalist in 1960 at the Summer Olympics in Rome and three-time World Heavyweight Champion.

Imothep Sfar, cat of the French cartoonist, screenwriter and director **Joann Sfar** (b. 1971). This sinuous gray Oriental with green eyes was evidently the muse for the central character of the *The Rabbi's Cat* comic book series, which, in 2011, was made into an animated film—the backstage video is a must.

Inga, a former cat mascot (along with **Nin**, **Jasper** and **Marty**) of the Mount Washington Observatory in New Hampshire.

Inigo and Jones, two tabby siblings taken in by Reverend **Simon Grigg** of St. Paul's, the "Actors' Church," in Covent Garden, London, which was designed between 1631 and 1633 by the architect Inigo Jones. Their main job is hunting mice, but they are also willing to handle religious duties. In particular, they excel at interrupting weddings—by jumping on the bride's train. And they regularly attend morning services: the fact that they are given breakfast immediately after that naturally has nothing to do with their devotion.

Itchy in *The Itchy & Scratchy Show*, a television show within a television show (*The Simpsons*) in which a black cat (Scratchy) is repeatedly killed by a blue mouse (Itchy)—like Tom and Jerry, but with more death.

Izzy the Cat, one of the over 50 felines of **Ernest Hemingway** (1899–1961), the American writer and Nobel Prize. The energetic tabby's full name was actually "Isabella the Catholic," in honor of the queen of Spain, consort of Ferdinand II and patroness of Christopher Columbus. This was a tribute to the cat's adventurous and bold character. Hemingway was first given a white six-toed cat, whom he named "Snowball," and most of the cats that later lived with him and continue, today, to reside in the Ernest Hemingway Home and Museum in Key West, Florida, are descendants of Snowball—and all polydactyl (felines with "extra" toes).
See also Boise, Uncle Wolfe and Sir Winston Churchill

for *Ikati* ('cat' in Zulu)

Also, *ikos* (in Central Bikol) and *iring* (in Cebuano). The coats of many breeds of domestic and stray cats feature patterns classified as "tabby." The word "tabby" is derived from the Latin *attabi*, while the Arabic word *attabiya* refers to the Attabiyah region in modern-day Iraq known for producing silk with motifs reminiscent of striped, variegated or calico "tabby" patterns.

Coat: stripes, dots or lines, usually with an M-shaped stripe on the forehead; mackerel, classic, spotted and ticked are common tabby patterns

Temperament: cats with tabby coats will have the personality traits of the breed to which they belong, but are also thought to be especially active and affectionate

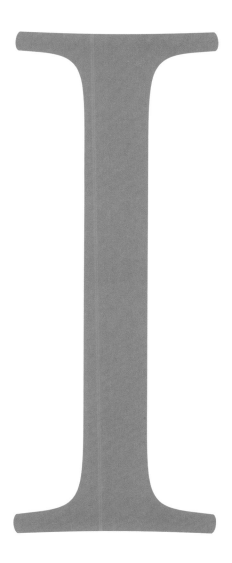

Invisible... like the Cheshire Cat ♣

[She] was a little startled by seeing the Cheshire Cat sitting on a bough of a tree a few yards off. The Cat only grinned when it saw Alice. It looked good-natured, she thought: still it had VERY long claws and a great many teeth, so she felt that it ought to be treated with respect.

"Cheshire Puss," she began, rather timidly, as she did not at all know whether it would like the name: However, it only grinned a little wider. "Come, it's pleased so far," thought Alice, and she went on. "Would you tell me, please, which way I ought to go from here?"

"That depends a good deal on where you want to get to," said the Cat.

"I don't much care where——" said Alice.

"Then it doesn't matter which way you go," said the Cat.

"——so long as I get SOMEWHERE," Alice added as an explanation.

"Oh, you're sure to do that," said the Cat, "if you only walk long enough."

Alice felt that this could not be denied, so she tried another question. "What sort of people live about here?"

"In THAT direction," the Cat said, waving its right paw round, "lives a Hatter: and in THAT direction," waving the other paw, "lives a March Hare. Visit either you like: they're both mad."

"But I don't want to go among mad people," Alice remarked.

"Oh, you can't help that," said the Cat, "we're all mad here. I'm mad. You're mad."

"How do you know I'm mad?" said Alice.

"You must be," said the Cat, "or you wouldn't have come here."

Alice didn't think that proved it at all; however, she went on. "And how do you know that you're mad?"

"To begin with," said the Cat, "a dog's not mad. You grant that?"

"I suppose so," said Alice.

"Well, then," the Cat went on, "you see, a dog growls when it's angry, and wags its tail when it's pleased. Now, I growl when I'm pleased, and wag my tail when I'm angry. Therefore, I'm mad."

"I call it purring, not growling," said Alice.

"Call it what you like," said the Cat. "Do you play croquet with the Queen to-day?"

"I should like it very much," said Alice, "but I haven't been invited yet."

"You'll see me there," said the Cat, and vanished.

Alice was not much surprised at this, she was getting so used to queer things happening. While she was looking at the place where it had been, it suddenly appeared again.

"By-the-by, what became of the baby?" said the Cat. "I'd nearly forgotten to ask."

"It turned into a pig," Alice quietly said, just as if it had come back in a natural way.

"I thought it would," said the Cat, and vanished again.

Alice waited a little, half expecting to see it again, but it did not appear, and after a minute or two she walked on in the direction in which the March Hare was said to live. "I've seen hatters before," she said to herself, "The March Hare will be much the most interesting, and perhaps as this is May it won't be raving mad—at least not so mad as it was in March." As she said this, she looked up, and there was the Cat again, sitting on a branch of a tree.

"Did you say 'pig,' or 'fig'?" said the Cat.

"I said 'pig,'" replied Alice, "and I wish you wouldn't keep appearing and vanishing so suddenly: You make one quite giddy."

"All right," said the Cat; and this time it vanished quite slowly, beginning with the end of the tail, and ending with the grin, which remained some time after the rest of it had gone.

"Well! I've often seen a cat without a grin," thought Alice, "but a grin without a cat! It's the most curious thing I ever saw in my life!"

Lewis Carroll, *Alice's Adventures in Wonderland*, London: Macmillan & Co., 1865.

♣The cat with the unforgettable smile who lives in Alice's
magical Wonderland.

Jake (also Zunar-J-5/9 Doric-4-7), the Martian Abyssinian star of the 1978 Disney movie *The Cat from Outer Space*, played by **Amber** and **Rumple**. This extraterrestrial cat "speaks," thanks to a special collar; the cat's voice in the movie is that of Ronnie Schell.
Dr. Wilson: You? That's you?
Jake: Well, it isn't the mouse.

Jeannie and Ptolemy, two of the cats of the late English astronomer **Sir Patrick Moore** CBE, FRS (1923–2012), who also wrote *Miaow! Cats Really are Nicer than People* (2012).

Jeoffry, cat of **Christopher Smart** (1722–71), an English poet who was confined to mental asylums between 1757 and 1763, during which period he wrote *Jubilate Agno*, arguably one of his best works. A section of the poem is a tribute to the cat who had been his companion during his confinement. "For I will consider my Cat Jeoffry. … / For when he takes his prey he plays with it to give it a chance. / For one mouse in seven escapes by his dallying. … / For he is of the tribe of Tiger."

Jezebel, the black-and-white cat of one of the residents of the spooky brownstone in the 1977 horror film *The Sentinel*.

Jones (1), *see Inigo*

Jones (2), the red cat and sole survivor, along with Ripley (Sigourney Weaver), in *Alien* (1979) by Ridley Scott.

James, one of the cats of the English writer and antiquarian **Oswald Barron** FSA (1868–1939). "James was the sort of cat to whom adventure calls … Pretty it was to see the sleek **Pippa** welcome back James from his battles, mewing about him, asking how he came by his scratches. James had no story to tell. He had fought and held his own … A slovenly cat was James, as ever I saw. Pippa, who will wash herself from ears to tail after eating the tail of a sardine, could never understand the fine carelessness of the male. I have seen her, in distress over his slovenliness, turn to and wash James and sleek out his fur. James bore her with humour; at such times his eye was like the eye of a man who is having his white tie properly tied for him by female hands."

Jeepers Creepers, one of the Siamese cats of the British American actress **Elizabeth Taylor** (1932–2011).
See also Marcus

Jenkins, a Siamese cat with a slipper fetish. His British owner, **Barbara Davies**, caught him red-handed as he hauled home a furry slipper bigger than he was. A few days later, he repeated his feat with the matching slipper.

Jerry, one of the cats of Freddie Mercury (1946–91), to whom the singer dedicated his solo album *Mr. Bad Guy* (1985). The dedication reads: "To my cat Jerry – also **Tom**, **Oscar** and **Tiffany**, and all the cat lovers across the universe – screw everybody else."

Jiji, the talking black cat of apprentice witch **Kiki** in Hayao Myazaki's 1989 animated film *Kiki's Delivery Service*.

Josephine, a white longhaired cat who, along with a seal-mitted male named **Daddy Warbucks** and a solid black cat called Blackie, is believed to have started the Ragdoll breed, registered with this name by her owner, **Ann Baker**. Like Josephine, her descendents typically go limp, like a ragdoll, when they're picked up.

Jellylorum, cat of the English poet, playwright and Nobel Laureate **T. S. Eliot** (1888–1965), and likely inspiration for Eliot's collection of poems, *Old Possum's Book of Practical Cats* (1939). Andrew Lloyd Webber's musical *Cats*, based on this collection, features a female character by the same name. Meanwhile, Eliot described his cat in a letter that he wrote to his godson Tom Faber in 1931: "I am glad you have a cat, but I do not believe it is so remarkable as my cat … There never was such a Lilliecat. Its name is Jellylorum, and its one idea is to be useful. For instance, it straightens the pictures, it does the grates, looks into the larder to see what's needed, and into the dustbin to see that nothing's wasted. And yet it is so little and small that it can sit on my ear!" (Andrew Lloyd Webber and John Napier, *Cats: The Book of the Musical, Based on "Old Possum's Book of Practical Cats" by T. S. Eliot*, New York, NY: Harcourt Brace Jovanovich, 1983)
See also Asparagus, Victoria and Wiscus

Jock, one of the many cats of **Sir Winston Churchill** (1874–1965), Prime Minister of the United Kingdom during World War II. The British civil servant Sir John ("Jock") Colville gave Jock, a ginger cat with a white spot on his chest, to Churchill for his 88th birthday. When Churchill died two years later, Jock stayed on at Chartwell, the Churchill family home—and a marmalade cat named "Jock" has resided at Chartwell ever since.
See also Nelson and Tango

Juliet, the Siamese of the American actor **Joe Mantegna** (b. 1947).

Julius, **Jay**, **Jethro**, brothers of Varjak Paw.

for *Javanese*

An Oriental Longhair that came about, in Great Britain, thanks to a Turkish Angora breeding program that included a Siamese cross. In 1979, the breed was named after an island of Indonesia due to its marked Oriental group characteristics, such as its wedge-shaped head.
Coat: soft and silky, longer on the tail; medium-haired, no undercoat
Temperament: affectionate

Black Jack ❧

In the days when that famous and learned man, Sir Richard Garnett, ruled over the Department of Printed Books in the British Museum, he was frequently visited by a cat who was generally known among the staff as 'Black Jack'.

He was a very handsome black creature, with a white shirt front and white paws, and whiskers of great length. He was fond of sitting on the desks in the Reading Room, and he never hesitated to ask a reader to hold open both folding doors when he wanted to go out into the corridor. Being shut in one of the newspaper rooms one Sunday, and being bored, he amused himself by sharpening his claws on the bindings of the volumes of newspapers, and it must be confessed did much damage. This brought down upon him the wrath of the officials, and he was banished from the library; the Clerk of the Works was ordered to get rid of him, and tried to do so, but failed, fot Black Jack had disappeared mysteriously. The truth was that two of the members of the staff arranged for him to be kept in safety in a certain place, and provided him with food and milk. An official report was written to the effect that Black Jack had disappeared, and he was 'presumed dead'; the bindings of the volumes of newspapers were repaired, and the official mind was once more at peace. A few weeks later Black Jack reappeared, and everyone was delighted to see him again; and the chief officials asked no questions!

Early in the spring of 1908 the Keeper of the Egyptian cat mummies in the British Museum was going down the steps of his official residence, when he saw Black Jack coming towards the steps and carrying something rather large in his mouth. He came to the steps and deposited his burden on the steps at the Keeper's feet and then turned and walked solemnly away. The something which he deposited on the steps was a kitten, and that kitten was later known to fame as 'Mike'.

E. A. WALLIS BUDGE, Sir, *"Mike," the Cat Who Assisted in Keeping the Main Gate of the British Museum from February* 1909 *to January* 1929, London: the author (printed by R. Clay & Sons, Ltd., Bungay, Suffolk), 1929.

❧The first furry "Keeper of Printed Books" (but shredder of newspaper volumes…) at the British Museum's Reading Room in London.

Kai, the ginger cat of **Patti Smith** (b. 1946), the American singer, poetess and artist. In Steven Sebring's documentary *Patti Smith: Dream of Life* (2008), Patti croons a verse from a 1968 song by the Italian singer-songwriter Fabrizio De André, *Amore che vieni, Amore che vai* (partly translated into English), to Kai, who responds with soulful purring.

Kare Kedi, the cat of the French author **Claude Farrère** (Frédéric-Charles Bargogne) (1876–1957). One night he awoke the writer with his meowing and started to stare at one of the walls in the room for no apparent reason. The following morning, the Frenchman discovered that his neighbor had been murdered in the very next room.

Katze, the black-and-white cat of Gustav Klimt (1862–1918), the Austrian artist and one of the founding members of the Vienna Secession movement.

Kerman, the travel companion—along with **Zeris**—of the British explorer and writer **A. Henry Savage Landor** (1865–1924) in *Across Coveted Lands*, vol. 2 (1902). "[On] the hump of the last camel of my caravan were perched, in a wooden box made comfortable with straw and cotton-wool, two pretty Persian kittens, aged respectively three weeks and four weeks, which I had purchased in Kerman, and which [proved] themselves to be the most wonderful and agreeable little travelling companions imaginable."

KinKin, the first of the Bengal breed.

Kitty Cat, the feline of the American singer **Janis Joplin** (1943–70).

Kinkwaneko, which means Golden Flower in Japanese, is the legendary name of the "golden-red" cats who, in Japanese folklore, have the supernatural powers that, in the West, are attributed to black cats—plus, the ability to turn themselves into beautiful women.

Miss Kitty, the cat of **Selina Kyle/ Catwoman** (Michelle Pfeiffer) in *Batman Returns* (1992) by Tim Burton.

Kallikrates, an orange Persian in the novel *Blind Alley* (1919) by the English author **Walter Lionel George** (1882–1926).

Kapok, Kiki-la-Doucette and **Kro**, some of the cats of **Sidonie-Gabrielle Colette** (1873–1954), the French author and cat connoisseur who wrote *Sept dialogues de bêtes* (1905), in which **Kiki** is the leading character, and *La Chatte* (1933), which features **Saha**.
See also Fanchette (p. 34)

Kaspar, the "wooden dinner guest" that has been at the Savoy Hotel Savoy in London since 1927. It is a 2-foot-high black cat in the Art Deco style, carved by the sculptor Basil Ionides, with the specific task of serving as the 14th guest if necessary to avoid having the unlucky number of 13 at a dinner table. His discreet and silent presence was said to have been particularly appreciated by Winston Churchill.

Kicia, the Dutch cat who accidentally boarded the Polish Navy's warship ORP *Burza* just before the start of World War II. The ship's commander considered the appearance of a cat to be a good omen and so Kicia was added to the crew list and housed in the non-commissioned officers' cabins at the bow of the ship, where she gave birth to six kittens. A little while later, during a powerful Atlantic storm, she moved her young family to the ship's stern, and, just a few days after that, ORP *Burza* was bombed, causing significant damage to the communal areas—including the cabin area from where Kicia had decided to relocate her kittens…

Kirlee, the quintessential Devon Rex. Parameters of the breed are based on its original characteristics: wavy coat, bat ears and a pixie-like face.

Kao K'o Kung (also Koko), the sensitive yet shrewd Siamese who, with his companion **Yum Yum**, helps reporter **James Qwilleran** solve countless crimes committed throughout the "Cat Who…" series by **Lilian Jackson Braun** (1913–2011), which totaled 29 murder mysteries, starting with *The Cat Who Could Read Backwards* (1966).

Karoun, the "king of cats" to whom **Jean Maurice Eugène Clément Cocteau** (1889-1963), the French poet, novelist, designer and director, dedicated *Drôle de ménage* (1948). His features inspired the makeup of the Beast in Cocteau's 1946 film *Beauty and the Beast*.

Katy, a Siamese cat from the town of Asbest in Russia, who, in 2003, was reported to weigh nearly 50 pounds (23 kilograms) and have a girth of 27.5 inches (70 cm).

Kiddo, the cat who joined the first attempt to fly across the Atlantic Ocean, aboard the airship *America* in 1910. The crew's navigator, Murray Simon, is said to have enlisted Kiddo, advising, "You must never cross the Atlantic in an airship without a cat—more useful to use than any barometer." Kiddo seems to have had other ideas, though, and the frightened feline's antics reputedly became the subject of the first wireless communication from an aircraft, with crew member Melvin Vaniman barking to a member of the support team back on land: "Roy, come and get this goddamn cat."

Kitty, *see Dinah*

Krazy Kat, the leading character in the most famous comic strip of World War I, created by the American cartoonist George Harriman (1880–1944). Because of the style of the illustrations and the use of slang, the comic strip's fans included the likes of James Joyce and E. E. Cummings.

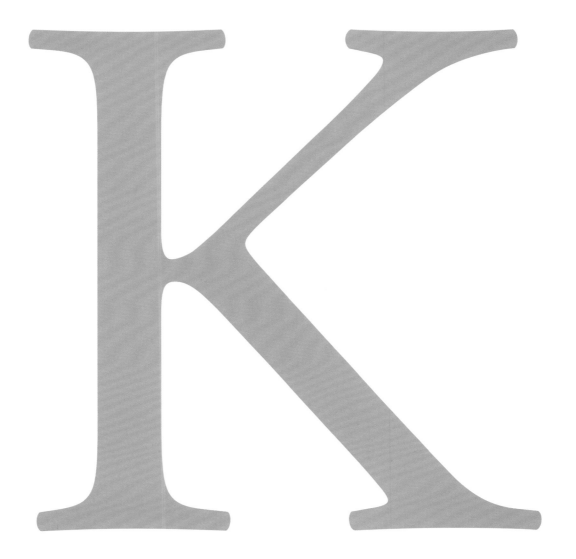

for *Korat*

Known in Thailand since the seventeenth century (Nakhon Ratchasima, or "Korat," is a province in the northeast of what was then Siam), the breed was recognized in the United States in 1966 and then in Great Britain in 1975. According to a Thai poem, the Korat has "eyes that glitter like dewdrops on lotus leaves."

Coat: short, light silver-tipped bluish gray

Temperament: sensitive, loyal and energetic

Kiki-la-Doucette ❦

[Toby-Chien complains about indigestion.]

Kiki-la-Doucette: ... you woke me up.

Toby-Chien: I felt uncomfortable. I was looking for help, a word of encouragement.

Kiki-la-Doucette: I don't know any digestive words. And when I think that, of the two of us, I'm the one people consider a nasty character! Just look at yourself, mate! The heat infuriates you, hunger makes you lose your mind, the cold paralyses you ...

Toby-Chien: I'm sensitive ...

Kiki-la-Doucette: More like a maniac.

Toby-Chien: No, I wouldn't say that. You! You're horribly selfish.

Kiki-la-Doucette: Maybe. The Two Legs—or you, try denying it—understand nothing about selfishness. The selfishness of Cats. ... That's what, in so many words, they have termed the instinct of preservation, reserved modesty, dignity, sacrifice, the enervating sacrifice that comes from the fact that it's impossible for them to understand us. Dog of little distinction, but without prejudices, can you understand me better? The Cat is a guest and not a toy. To be honest, what sort of times are we living in?! Are the Two Legs—He and She—the only ones with a right to grieve, to rejoice, to lick their plates, scream, run around the house in a foul mood? I have MY tantrums, MY sadness, my changeable appetite, my hours of dreamy seclusion when I cut myself off from the world...

Toby-Chien (*attentive and conscientious*): I'm listening to you but have a hard time following, because your discourse is complicated and a bit over my head. You astonish me. Do they regularly get upset about your moodiness? You meow: they open the door for you. You lie on the paper, the sacred paper HE writes on: HE moves or—wonder of wonders—leaves you the page you've ruined anyway. You walk, wrinkling your nose, waving your tail about sharply, and visibly looking for mischief: SHE watches you and laughs, and HE announces, "The walk of devastation". So? What are you complaining about?

Kiki-la-Doucette (*in bad faith*): I'm not complaining. Well, psychological subtleties will always go over your head.

Toby-Chien: Don't talk so fast. It takes me time to understand... It seems to me...

Kiki-la-Doucette (*scoffing*): Not so fast: your digestion could suffer.

Toby-Chien (*the irony lost on him*): You're right. I'm having a hard time expressing myself today. There. It seems that, of the two of us, you're the favorite. And yet you're the one who complains.

Kiki-la-Doucette: Canine logic! ... The more I get, the more I want.

Toby-Chien: But that's wrong! It's a lack of discretion!

Kiki-la-Doucette: No. I have a right to everything.

Toby-Chien: Everything? What about me?

Kiki-la-Doucette: You lack nothing, I suppose.

Toby-Chien: Nothing? I don't know. The times I feel happiest, I feel like crying so hard that my chest tightens, my eyes go misty... my heart suffocates me. In those minutes of anxiety, I'd like to be sure that everything alive loves me, that there isn't a sad dog behind any door anywhere in the world, and that nothing bad will ever happen...

Kiki-la-Doucette (*teasing*): And then something bad happens?

COLETTE, *Sept dialogues de bêtes*, Paris: Mercure de France, 1905.

❦The sublime Chartreux who, together with the tiger-striped brindle French bulldog Toby-Chien, are the leading characters of *Dialogues de bêtes*, in which conversations between the two have been "transcribed" by Colette.

Laurel Queen, the British shorthair of **Charles Henry Lane**, author of one of the first manuals on cat breeds—and more… *Rabbits, Cats and Cavies. Descriptive Sketches Of All Recognised Exhibition Varieties With Many Original Anecdotes* (1903). The winner of almost every English beauty contest for cats in 1910, Laurel Queen headed a Laurel dynasty, including **Laurel Tiddles**, who is described in *Rabbits, Cats and Cavies* as follows: "Laurel Tiddles, the black, had a habit which would be trying to nervous persons, but, fortunately, she nearly always selected me for its exercise. If she caught sight of me walking anywhere about the place, she would run at top speed and spring on my shoulder from behind, and usually knocked off my hat with the vigour of her expressions of delight at her feat."
See also Victor et Yellow Boy

Lil Bub, a feline star of the Internet despite—or perhaps thanks to—her many genetic mutations, which give her a very distinctive appearance. The runt of the litter, she is polydactyl, toothless, and her tongue always hangs out, although this has not affected her big appetite. The documentary *Lil Bub & Friendz* (2013) won an award at the 2013 Tribeca Film Festival, New York, at which point Lil Bub met Robert De Niro. Most of the profits from the sales of merchandise and public appearances has been donated to animal shelters.

Loulou, little Portuguese Angora of **François Edouard Joachim Coppée** (1842–1908), who shared the attentions of the French poet and playwright (and a member of the jury at the first cat show held in Paris) with the elderly **Zézé** and the insatiable **Mistigris**.

Lucifer, the stepsisters' mean cat in Walt Disney's animated film *Cinderella* (1950).

Lu Lu *see Wong Wong*

Lux, one of the cats of Agnes Repplier (1855–1950), the American essayist who wrote *The Fireside Sphinx* (1901), devoted entirely to cats.

Midnight Louie, the black cat and hardboiled private investigator probing the crimes of Las Vegas, helping his human companion Temple Barr solve them, and narrating his version of the facts in Carole Nelson Douglas's novels. The eponymous series debuted in 1992 with *Catnap* and now boasts 25 titles. "When I call myself an 'alphacat,' some think I am merely asserting my natural feline male dominance, but no. I merely reference the fact that since I debuted in *Catnap* and *Pussyfoot*, I then commenced to a title sequence that is as sweet and simple as B to Z."
See also Yvette

Lucius Lyndon (formerly **Lucinda Virginia**), the neurotic head of the "collection" of strays taken in by Diane Lovejoy (he was followed by **Lydia**, **Leo**, **Linus**, **L.B.**, **Alvar**, **Lillie**, T.J., **Perkins** and **Miss Tommie**) described in *Cat Lady Chronicles*. "My steady routines were thrown for a loop when, twelve years ago, I found an emaciated feline in our backyard. I fell in love with the cat we eventually named Lucius and discovered that I did not subscribe to the power of one. More cats arrived. Many more followed. Many more stayed."

Le Chat, the cat "*par excellence*" of **Pierre Loti** (pseudonym of Julien Viaud) (1850–1923), the French novelist and navy officer. This four-year-old Siamese boasted "superior intelligence and an extraordinary memory." He was also "odd, a little unbalanced. Very great lord. Exceedingly affectionate and gentle, he offers me long discussions."
See also Belaud (2) and Ratonne

Lilith, the favorite black cat of the French symbolist poet **Stéphane Mallarmé** (1842–98). His friend, the American painter James Abbott McNeill Whistler tried to portray her, but managed to complete only a rapid sketch before she ran off to hide under the bed. "There are moments in which Lilith becomes a person, instants of intimacy in which her head [is like that] of a black women, minutes in which, suddenly, before my astonished gaze, the cat head turns into the face of an idol."
See also Neige

Lilliput, *see Frätzibutzi*

Limbo, the cat of the English writer Aldous Huxley (1894–1963) who was well known for his dystopian novels. *Limbo* was also the title of Huxley's first collection of short fiction (1920). "If you want to be a psychological novelist and write about human beings, the best thing you can do is keep a pair of cats."

Lily, the white and "very well behaved" cat of **Samuel Johnson** (1709–84), English critic, lexicographer and writer.
See also Hodge and Oscar

Logos, the cat of the French philosopher **Jacques Derrida** (1930–2004).

Lucifer (black as coal, of course), **Ludovic-le-Cruel** (the savage rat exterminator) and **Ludoviska** (of Polish descent), three of the fourteen cats of **Armand Jean Du Plessis** (1585–1642), cardinal and duke of Richelieu. The French statesman was always surrounded by his cats, setting aside an entire room for them and feeding them pâté morning and night.
See also Félimare, Perruque and Racan

Lucky Prince, *see Snowbell*

for *LaPerm*

The first example of this rex breed, with fur like a permanent wave hairstyle (hence the name), was born in a barn in Oregon in 1982 as a result of spontaneous genetic mutation.
Coat: short- or medium-haired, with curls and ringlets, and the fluffy texture of mohair
Temperament: very affectionate, clownish, with a tendency to climb onto people's shoulders or follow them around as a dog would

Sir John Langbourne[❈]

The British philosopher Jeremy Bentham was very fond of animals, particularly "pussies," as he called them, when they had domestic virtues, although he had no special affection for cats in general. He had one, however, about which he used to boast that he had "made a man of him," and whom he was wont to invite to eat macaroni at his own table. This puss got knighted, and rejoiced in the name of Sir John Langbourne.

In his early days, "Sir John" was frisky, inconsiderate and, to tell the truth, a somewhat profligate gentleman; and had, according to the report of his patron, the habit of seducing light and giddy young ladies, of his own species, into the garden of Queen's Square Place: but, tired at last, like Solomon, of pleasures and vanities, he became sedate and thoughtful—took to the church, laid down his knightly title and was installed as "The Reverend John Langbourne." He gradually obtained a great reputation for sanctity and learning, and a doctoral degree was duly conferred upon him. When I knew him, in his declining days, he bore no other name than The Reverend Sir John Langbourne , D.D. (Doctor of Divinity): and he was alike conspicuous for his gravity and philosophy. Great respect was invariably shown His Reverence: and it was supposed that he was not far off a mitre when old age interfered with his hopes and honors. He departed amidst the regrets of his many friends, and was gathered to his fathers, and to eternal rest, in a cemetery in Milton's garden.

CHRISTABEL ABERCONWAY (Baroness), *A Dictionary of Cat Lovers: XV Century B.C.–XX Century A.D.*, London: Michael Joseph, 1968 (1949), p. 56.

❈The cat of the philosopher and animal rights advocate Jeremy Bentham (1748–1832), described here by Sir John Bowring, Bentham's friend and literary executor.

Macek, the cat of the American scientist **Nikola Tesla** (1856–1943) whose electrostatic coat may be credited with some of the main discoveries regarding electromagnetism.

Marie *see Thomas O'Malley*

Marramaquiz and **Micifuf**, *see Zapaquilda* (p. 114)

Matilda, a Ragdoll and the "most famous guest" of the Algonquin Hotel, New York, who answers emails sent to matildaalgonquincat@ algonquinhotel.com. At her seventh birthday party, in 2002, she surprised her 150 "closest friends" in attendance by jumping on the cake rather than simply blowing out those candles… *See also Hamlet*

Mike, "the Cat Who Assisted in Keeping the Main Gate of the British Museum from February 1909 to January 1929." Mike was introduced into service by the "Reading Room cat" **Black Jack** (*see* p. 50).

Minette, one of the cats of **Gottfried Mind** (1768–1814), the Swiss-born artist referred to as the "Raphael of Cats."

Minouche (2) and **Coussi**, the cats of the French painter **Henri Matisse** (1869–1954).

Mooch, the big-nosed little black cat who loves pink socks, has been the inseparable companion of the dog Earl since 1994, in the comic strip *Mutts* by **Patrick McDonnell**.

Murr, philosopher cat of the German Romantic author **E. T. A. Hoffmann** (1776–1822), and co-author of *The Life and Opinions of the Tomcat Murr* (1820–22).

Magnificat, the black-and-white cat of **Philip K. Dick** (1928–82)—the author of *Do Androids Dream of Electric Sheep?* (1968), which inspired the movie *Blade Runner* (1982), had more wives than cats (five versus two).

Matterhorn is the name of the cat who, at the age of four months, ascended the eponymous mountain (14,691 feet) in the Swiss Alps on September 6, 1950, accompanying a group of mountain climbers who were astonished all the way up to the summit… and back.

Mimi, *see Rosa Luxemburg*

Minnaloushe, a black cat belonging to the family of **Maud Gonne**, muse of the Irish poet **W. B. Yeats** (1865–1939). The cat was immortalized in his poem "The Cat and the Moon" (1919)

Mitsou, the white Persian of **Marilyn Monroe** (1926–62). The American actress confessed that she had numerous problems finding a vet, because, when she would call, saying, "I'm Marilyn Monroe and my cat is about to have a litter," they would invariably suspect it to be a prank call and hang up on her.

Morris, formerly **Luky**, the first of the talking orange tabbies made famous by the ad for 9Lives cat food, was found in a Chicago animal shelter in 1967. "The Clark Gable of cats" died in 1978.

Mysouff I and **Mysouff II**, the cats of the French novelist **Alexandre Dumas**, *père* (1802–70). The former had a "canine vocation" and the latter devoured 500 francs worth of rare exotic birds. Put on trial by the author of *The Three Musketeers*, thanks to the pleadings of Nogent Saint-Laurent in his defense, Mysouff II was sentenced for a lesser crime due to the extenuating circumstance of being young and thus easily influenced.

Marcus, the Siamese cat **Liz Taylor** (1932–2011) gave **James Dean** (1931–1955) when they were filming *Giant* (1956). Instructions for Marcus's care included a recipe —1 x teaspoon of white Karo [corn syrup], 1 x big can of evaporated milk ("equal part boiled water or distilled water"), 1 x egg yolk ("mix and chill")—complete with serving suggestion ("Don't feed him meat or formula cold").

Marshmoff, the black cat of Frank Zappa (1940–93) who crouched on the shoulders of the American musician on the cover of his 1987 album *London Symphony Orchestra, Vol. 2*.

Menegheto, the white cat with tiger stripes on his head and the nape of his neck who appears in many paintings by the Italian artist Jacopo Bassano (1510–92).

Mimsie the Cat, born in 1968, started her film career with a yawn… the one used by MTM Enterprises, to parody Metro-Goldwyn-Mayer's roaring lion.

Minou (1), the cat of the French novelist George Sand (1804–76); the two of them would apparently eat from the same breakfast crockery.

Minou (2), the Siamese of a young Pablo Picasso (1881–1973). the friendship between the Spanish artist and his cat, which started over a stolen sausage.

Mokol, the cat who can, through the sunglasses he wears, reveal people's true natures—specifically, their feelings expressed as colors in the Czech film *The Cassandra Cat* (1963)

Moortje, the black cat that **Anne Frank** (1929–45) had to leave behind when she went into hiding in 1942, and **Mouchi**, the cat of **Peter van Pels**, who was also confined to the secret annex with Anne and her family. Also at the house in Amsterdam was a chubby cat called **Moffie** (named after pig-shaped cookies known as Moffen).

The Master's Cat, *see Williamina* (p. 102)

Micetto, a gray-and-ginger tabby born in the Raphael Rooms at the Vatican. He was raised by **Pope Leo XII** (1760–1829), on whose lap he would sit during audiences. Micetto was later bequeathed to **François René de Chateaubriand** (1768–1848), the French writer, statesman and ambassador to Rome, who took the papal puss back with him to Paris in 1829.

Minouche (1), the white female cat who was a favorite of **Émile Zola** (1840–1902) and was also known as "la Joie de Vivre" (a Zola's 1884 novel).

Muezza, purportedly the favorite cat of the prophet **Muhammad** (570–632). According to legend, when the prophet found Muezza asleep on a prayer robe he wished to wear, he cut the sleeve off rather than disturb the cat.

for *Maine Coon*

This was the first natural long-haired breed to appear in the United States—in Maine—and one theory of its origin goes back to 1770. Its tabby coat and long bushy tail erroneously led some people to believe it was a cross between a cat and a raccoon. *Coat*: medium-haired, dense, with a pronounced ruff around the neck and tufted paws; more than 60 combinations of colors and coat patterns have been recognized *Temperament*: balanced and reactive; prefers high places so it can monitor its surroundings; loves to play with water; "trills" rather than meowing

Madame Théophile❖

One day a friend of mine, who was going out of town for a few days, entrusted his parrot to me with the request that I would take care of it during his absence. The bird, feeling strange in my house, had climbed, helping himself with his beak, to the very top of his perch, and, looking pretty well bewildered, rolled round his eyes, which resembled the gilt nails on arm-chairs, and wrinkled the whitish membrane that served him for eyelids. Madame Théophile had never seen a parrot, and she was evidently much puzzled by the strange bird. Motionless as an Egyptian mummified cat in its network of bands, she gazed upon it with an air of profound meditation, and put together whatever she had been able to pick up of natural history on the roofs, in the courtyard and the garden. Her thoughts were reflected in her shifting glance, and I was able to read in it the result of her examination: "It is unmistakably a chicken."

Having reached this conclusion, she sprang from the table on which she had posted herself to make her investigations, and crouched down in one corner of the room, flat on her stomach, her elbows out, her head low, her muscular backbone on the stretch, like the black panther in Gérôme's painting watching gazelles on their way to the drinking-place.

The parrot followed her movements with feverish anxiety, fluffing out its feathers, rattling its chain, lifting its foot and moving its claws, and sharpening its beak upon the edge of its seed-box. Its instinct warned it that an enemy was preparing to attack it.

The eyes of the cat, fixed upon the bird with an intensity that had something of fascination in it, plainly said in a language well understood of the parrot and absolutely intelligible: "Green though it is, that chicken must be good to eat."

I watched the scene with much interest, prepared to interfere at the proper time. Madame Théophile had gradually crawled nearer; her pink nose was working, her eyes were half closed, her claws were protruded and then drawn in. She thrilled with anticipation like a gourmet sitting down to enjoy a truffled pullet; she gloated over the thought of the choice and succulent meal she was about to enjoy, and her senses were tickled by the idea of the exotic dish that was to be hers.

Suddenly she arched her back like a bow that is being drawn, and a swift leap landed her right on the perch. The parrot, seeing the danger upon him, unexpectedly called out in a deep, sonorous bass voice: "Have you had your breakfast, Jack?"

The words filled the cat with indescribable terror; and she leapt back. The blast of a trumpet, the smash of a pile of crockery, or a pistol-shot fired by her ear would not have dismayed the feline to such an extent. All her ornithological notions were upset.

"And what did you have?—A royal roast," went on the bird.

The cat's expression clearly meant: "This is not a bird; it's a man; it speaks."

"When of claret I've drunk my fill, the pot-house whirls and is whirling still," sang out the bird with a deafening voice, for it had at once perceived that the terror inspired by its speech was its surest means of defense.

The cat looked at me questioningly, and, my reply proving unsatisfactory, she sneaked under the bed, and refused to come out for the rest of the day.

Théophile Gautier, "My Private Menagerie," in F. C. de Sumichrast (Trans., Ed.),
The Works of Théophile Gautier, vol. 19, online, Project Gutenberg, 2009 (first published, 1902), 30760.

❖The feline "wife" of Théophile Gautier, so called because
she shared "conjugal intimacy" with the writer, sleeping at
the foot of his bed, dreaming on his armchair as he wrote,
accompanying him during his walks in the garden…

Nadjem, thought to be the cat of **Puimre**, an official in Ancient Egypt during the reigns of Hatshepsut (1508–1458 B.C.) and Thutmose III (1481–1425 B.C.). "Nadjem" (it can be translated to "dear one" or "star") was found etched on the walls of Piumre's tomb in the ancient city of Thebes, which may be the first instance of a cat's "pet name".

Nelly, cat of the English poet **Hartley Coleridge** (1796–1849), eldest son of Samuel Taylor Coleridge, nephew of Robert Southey.

Nelson, the large gray cat of **Sir Winston Churchill** (1874–1965), the English statesman who served as prime minister during World War II. He was named in honor of Admiral Horatio Nelson, because he valorously chased away a huge dog in front of the Admiralty House. In 1940, Churchill brought him to 10 Downing Street, where Nelson saw off "Munich Mouser," the resident cat of the previous administration. In 1943, Churchill was forced to convalesce in bed due to a serious bout of flu. As Nelson cuddled by his feet, Churchill pointed out to one of his ministers, "This cat does more for the war effort than you do. He acts as a hot water bottle and saves fuel and power."
See also Jock and Tango

New Boy, the Siamese cat that, in 1946, the British actor **Laurence Olivier** (1907–89) gave to his wife **Vivien Leigh** (1913–67), the unforgettable Scarlett O'Hara in the film *Gone with the Wind* (1939). New Boy, named for the New Theatre in London where Olivier often acted, traveled regularly with the couple and accompanied them to the theater as a good-luck charm. Leigh, who had previously owned a black-and-white stray named Tissy, said, "Once you have kept a Siamese cat you would never have any other kind. They make wonderful pets and are so intelligent they follow you around like little dogs." New Boy was succeeded by Armando, identical in every way, including a costly collar bought in Paris.

Nicholas, the Ragdoll cat of **Dusty Springfield** (Mary O'Brien, 1939–99), the English singer famous for *You Don't Have to Say You Love Me* (1966). In her will, she left detailed instructions for Nicholas's care—including a note that he was to be serenaded with her songs.

Nigger Man, the unfortunate name of the cat of American "weird fiction" author **H. P. Lovecraft** (1890–1937) when he was a boy, and also of the cat in his short story *The Rats in the Walls* (1924) (the cat's name was changed to "Black Tom" in a later reprinting). The writer clearly shows that he was a passionate connoisseur of felines in his 1926 essay "Cats and Dogs": "Dogs are the hieroglyphs of blind emotion, inferiority, servile attachment, and gregariousness—the attributes of commonplace, stupidly passionate, and intellectually and imaginatively underdeveloped men. Cats are the runes of beauty, invincibly, wonder, pride, freedom, coldness, self-sufficiency, and dainty individuality—the qualities of sensitive, enlightened, mentally developed, pagan, cynical, poetic, philosophic, dispassionate, reserved, independent, Nietzschean, unbroken, civilized, master-class men. The dog is a peasant and the cat is a gentlemen. ... The dog gives, but the cat is."

Napoleon, a meteorologist cat who resided in Baltimore, Maryland, in the 1930s. According to his owner, before a rainstorm, Napoleon would lie on the floor, belly down, with his head between his outstretched legs. During a long dry spell with no end in sight, he once again laid down in this portentous position, so his owner called the local newspaper to let them know it would rain soon. No one believed her, but, after a downpour promptly ensued, the paper published the climatic cat's weather predictions for the next six years.

Nega, one of two magical white cats—the other is Posi—watching over use of the magical, transformative powers granted to young Yū in the animated television series *Creamy Mami, the Magic Angel* (1983–84).

Nepia, one of the 13 cats at Normanton House, the family home of **Sir Oliver Lodge** (1851–1940), the English physicist who pioneered wireless telegraphy. The Normanton felines—the other 12 being Barny, Grief, Oliver Twist, Parker, Patsy, Pondicherry, Puddy, Sarah, Stella, Tiger, Tissy and Zulu—were portrayed in great detail by Lodge's secretary, Miss Alney. Nepia is the "mathematical" cat with a calculating eye.

Neige, the snow-white Angora of the French poet **Stéphane Mallarmé** (1842–98) and the mother of Frimas, another of Mallarmé's menagerie.
See also Lilith

Nermal, "the world's cutest kitten," as Garfield's friend has proudly defined himself since first appearing in the comic strip in 1979.

Nestor, the French cat shot for treason during World War I for fraternizing with German soldiers (who had named him "Felix"). His story is told in the Christian Carion film *Joyeux Noël* (*Merry Christmas*) (2005) about the Christmas truce of 1914 between the trenches of French, German and Scottish soldiers.

Nini, the famous Angora of Venice, where the **Borgato family** that owned the café across from the Basilica di Santa Maria Gloriosa dei Frari named their business in his honor. The *Albo d'oro* (roll of honor) collected signatures of all the illustrious figures who came to admire him, from Pope Leo XIII to the Czar of Russia, and Verdi even dedicated Act III of *La Traviata* (1853) to him.

Nora, the big gray pianist with a bossy temperament but unquestionable musical talent. Named after the British-born Mexican artist, Leonora Carrington, Nora was adopted in New Jersey by **Betsy Alexander**, a piano instructor, and is now a global Internet star.

Nyx, the bluish-gray cat at the County Public Library in Chesterfield, Virginia. Born with deformed eyes, she owes her name to the Greek goddess of the night. Extremely affectionate and perfectly at easy amidst the bookshelves and with people, she is the favorite pet of all the librarians.

for *Norwegian Forest Cat*

As its name suggests, the breed was common in the forests of Norway, and, according to legend, was a sacred passenger on Viking ships. By the early twentieth century, it had become rare in its native country, but, in the 1970s, a national breeding program ensured its comeback; breeding began in Great Britain in 1973 and in the United States in 1979.
Coat: medium-haired, dense, double coat; water repellent, suited to cold climates
Temperament: independent but sociable; needs plenty of room to wander and climb

Norton ❧

When we arrived at the restaurant, Bistro d'Albert, a charming and perfect place that could exist only in France, Norton was greeted the way I imagine Ike was when he arrived at the Champs-Élysées immediately following D-Day. He was given, as he always is, his own chair, which he settled into quite comfortably. The owner, a typical somewhere-over-forty-year-old blonde Frenchwoman for whom you'd happily give the rest of your life if she'd only so much as smile at you, smiled up a storm. But not at me, oh no. At my innocent-looking furry friend, who, just to annoy me, I'm sure, purred like a motorboat, rolled over on his back, and practically begged the owner and all of her gorgeous waitresses to come over and scratch his stomach, which, of course, they did. Meanwhile, I was doing my best to order a kir, but I couldn't get anyone to look at me.

PETER GETHERS, *A Cat Abroad: The Further Adventures of Norton, the Cat Who Went to Paris, and His Human,* New York: Fawcett Columbine, 1993, p. 2.

❧The irresistible globetrotting Scottish Fold of the American writer Peter Gethers (b. 1955), the central character in the autobiographical novel *The Cat Who Went to Paris* (New York: Crown Publishers 1991; republished in 2009 (London: Ebury) as *A Cat Called Norton*), and such a literary celebrity that he merited two sequels, *A Cat Abroad* and *The Cat Who'll Live Forever*, co-starring Gethers.

Octavius, the "octave" of the (many) cats of **Gertrude Jekyll** (1843–1932), English garden designer and writer—and a true cat lady. She had from five or six cats up to a number comprising two digits (see p. 106), including Chloe, Crevette, Pinkieboy, Tabby, Tittlebat, Patty, Toozle, Tavy, Tommy, Mittens and Maggie.

Oliver Twist, the yellow-eyed black cat of the English physicist **Sir Oliver Lodge** (1851–1940). As a kitten, he loved to burst in on the professor's scholarly discussions about relativity, disturbing Zulu, another of Lodge's many felines, as he listened intently.
See also Nepia

Orangey, the tabby who starred in a dozen films in the 1950s and 1960s, including the role of "Cat" in *Breakfast at Tiffany's* (1961), which won him his *second* PATSY Award (Picture Animal Top Star of the Year), the equivalent of an Oscar for animals. Despite his lovely appearance, one of the producers described Orangey as "the world's meanest cat." Although he acted his parts with great professionalism, he would scamper off the set as soon as the scene was done, blocking production until he could be found again. In fact, his trainer **Frank Inn** had guard dogs set up at the studio exits.
See also Rhubarb

Oscar (1), the ship's cat nicknamed "Unsinkable Sam." Rescued by the crew of the British destroyer HMS *Cossack* after the German ship he was on, the *Bismarck*, was sunk on May 27, 1941, a few months later he was saved again by the crew of the British aircraft carrier HMS *Ark Royal* when the *Cossack* was torpedoed by a German submarine on October 24. When, in turn, the *Ark Royal* was torpedoed and sank in November of that year, just a few miles from Gibraltar, Oscar was brought to the base and remained there until a courageous ship heading to Belfast decided to run the risk of taking him aboard…. Oscar reached his destination and lived in a seaman's home until his death in 1955. Although his portrait is preserved at the National Maritime Museum in Greenwich, some doubt the entire story—perhaps because the painting shows a black-and-white cat, but a photograph shows a tabby!

O Toyo, the name of the beautiful girl killed by the Vampire Cat of Nabéshima so he could assume her form, in one of the stories told by **Baron Redesdale** (1837–1916), writing under the pen name of A. B. Mitford (*Tales of Old Japan*, 1871).

The Old Lady, the "silver tabby, good in colour and marking" of **Harrison Weir** (1824–1906), founder and first president of the English National Cat Club, in 1887, and promoter of the first cat show in Great Britain, held in July, 1871 at the Crystal Palace in London.

Olly, a one-eared ginger-and-white cat at Manchester Airport in England, named after Olympic House, the airport's main office, where "he" (she turned out to be an "Olivia") was first spotted in 2007. Olly was adopted by the airport staff and soon became their mascot—she has even had a plane named after her.

Orion, the red-and-white cat with a galaxy attached to his collar in the film *Men in Black* (1997) directed by Barry Sonnenfeld.

Oliver Hoyt Goldberg, one of the cats of American actress **Whoopi Goldberg** (b. 1935). Following the 2008 elections, the actress had the cat "write" to Barack Obama to suggest that, instead of getting a puppy, his family get a "self-sufficient, tidy and clean" cat for the White House.

Orangello, the world-famous cat artist. A limited edition of his painting *Beam Me Up* is exhibited at the Philip Wood Gallery in Berkeley, California, an international gallery that, since 1994, has specialized in artwork produced by cats.

Orlando the Marmalade Cat, the ginger tabby starring in the 18 children's books created by the English illustrator **Kathleen Hale** (1898–2000), first published in 1938.

Oscar (2), cat of the English wood engraver and illustrator **Yvonne Skargon** (1931–2010), who is portrayed in *The Importance of Being Oscar* (1988), a published collection of Skargon's engravings,

Otello, *see Desdemona*

Otto, the late, much-loved Turkish Van of **Andrew Lloyd Webber** (b. 1948), the English composer who wrote the musical *Cats*, which debuted at the New London Theatre on 11 May 1981 and went on to become one of the most successful shows in the world.

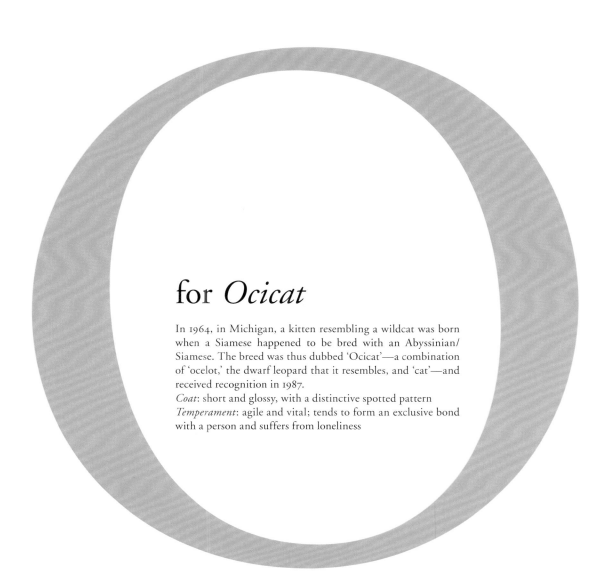

for *Ocicat*

In 1964, in Michigan, a kitten resembling a wildcat was born when a Siamese happened to be bred with an Abyssinian/Siamese. The breed was thus dubbed 'Ocicat'—a combination of 'ocelot,' the dwarf leopard that it resembles, and 'cat'—and received recognition in 1987.

Coat: short and glossy, with a distinctive spotted pattern
Temperament: agile and vital; tends to form an exclusive bond with a person and suffers from loneliness

Ovid ❖

For a considerable time afterwards, an evil fortune attended all our attempts at re-establishing a cattery. Ovid disappeared and Virgil died of some miserable distemper. You and your cousin [Hartley Coleridge] are answerable for these names: the reason which I could find for them were, in the former case, the satisfactory one that Ovid might be presumed to be a master in the art of love; and, in the latter, the probable one that something like Maro [Publius Vergilius Maro] might be detected in the said Virgil's notes of courtship.

ROBERT SOUTHEY, *Memoir of the Cats of Greta Hall*, in the form of a letter to his daughter, Edith May, Keswick, 18 Jan. 1824, in ROBERT SOUTHEY and JOHN WOOD WARTER (Ed.) *The Doctor*, VII, London: Longman, Brown, Green, and Longmans, 1847, pp. 582–596.

❖ One of the innumerable cats owned by the English poet and prose writer Robert Southey (1774–1843), which he raised in the family home (Greta Hall, Keswick, in the Lake District) and which were often described in his letters. Ovid—along with Othello, Virgil and the Zombi—was part of Keswick's prevailing "black dynasty."

Pai-hsueh Ku (Miss White Snow), thought to be China's earliest "missing cat." She is cited in a notice reporting her disappearance from the home of **Yu Ta-Po**, citizen of Pien-liang (now Kaifeng), in Honan (Henan) Province, in the tenth century A.D.

Pepper the Cat was cast in 18 movies between 1913 and 1921, including *Down on the Farm*, a 1920 silent comedy by Mack Sennett (United Artists, 1920).

Perruque and **Racan**, two of the cats of **Armand Jean Du Plessis**, cardinal and duke of Richelieu (1585–1642), owe their name to the fact that they were born in the wig ("*perruque*" in French) of the scholar Honorat de Bueil, seigneur de Racan (1589–1670). Another two of his cats, **Pyrame** and **Thisbé**, were so named because they would fall asleep in an embrace, like ill-fated pair in Ovid's *Metamorphoses*.
See also Félimare and Lucifer

Pitou, cat of the French painter and co-founder of Fauvism **André Derain** (1880–1954).

Polly, one of countless beloved cats of the American director, screenwriter and producer **Stanley Kubrick** (1928–99). Kubrick suspected that Polly had supernatural powers, as she seemed to know when the director wanted to comb her hair and cut any knots, and would always go hide under the bed.

Purdoe, the name that Miss **Eliza Mary Anne Savage** (d. 1885) gave the cat she received from the writer **Samuel Butler** (1835–1902), with whom she enjoyed an extensive epistolary relationship revolving chiefly around cats.

Purrie, the cat of David Bowie (b. 1947), the "duke" of English pop culture and, not without coincidence, the author of *Cat People*, the title song of the 1982 erotic horror of the same name starring the fabulously feline Nastassja Kinski.

Palémon, the green-eyed tabby who held office in the study of the French literary critic, essayist and poet **Charles-Augustin Sainte-Beuve** (1804–69), and who had a special fondness for the poet Théophile Gautier (as did Sainte-Beuve, who reviewed Gautier's work most enthusiastically), never tiring of his caresses.

Peter, the cat of **Emily** and **Louis Wain** (1860–1939), and a model for Louis's hundreds of drawings of anthropomorphized cats, including those featured in *A Kittens' Christmas Party* (1886). According to H. G. Wells, "English cats that do not look and live like Louis Wain cats are ashamed of themselves."

Piccolo, one of the cats of the German theologian, philosopher, musicologist and physician **Albert Schweitzer** (1875–1965). If Piccolo fell asleep on the scholar's papers and someone needed them, that someone had to wait until the cat woke up.

Procope, beloved cat of the French painter **Jean-Auguste-Dominique Ingres** (1780–1867).

Püffchen, one of the cats of **Carmen Sylva** (Elisabeth of Wied) (1843–1916). The Queen of Romania would keep him on her lap, tucked into a fur bag, when she played the piano, in the hopes of teaching him to appreciate music. Every time, Püffchen would demonstrate his enjoyment… by running away.
See Frätzibutzi and Vulpi

Pushkin, the dark chocolate cat of the English writer and philosopher John McTaggart Ellis (1866–1925). "Miss Stawell commented to him, 'I believe if there was only one cosy chair in the room you would give it to Pushkin, and take the floor yourself.' McTaggart's answer: 'Of course I would.'"

Pyewacket, the Siamese cat and familiar spirit of **Gillian Holroyd** (Kim Novak's witch character) in *Bell, Book and Candle* (1958), a film directed by Richard Quine.

Pangur Bán, the cat—probably white (*bán* in Old Gaelic)—who provided companionship to an Irish monk who was transcribing the *Letters of Saint Paul* in a monastery in Austria in the ninth century. The cat inspired the poem *Pangur Bán*, one of the earliest written in Old Gaelic, in which the monk compares their mutual nocturnal labor:
"I and Pangur Bán my cat,
"'Tis a like task we are at:
"Hunting mice is his delight,
"Hunting words I sit all night."

Philip Argent and **St. Philip Neri**, two of the cats of the English religion and spirituality writer **Evelyn Underhill** (1875–1941).

Pippa, *see James*

Pluto, the unfortunate protagonist of **Edgar Allan Poe**'s terrifying short story "The Black Cat" (1843).
See also Catarina

Pudlenka, one of the cats of the Czech writer **Karel Čapek** (1890–1938). In his book *I Had a Dog and a Cat* (1940), Čapek is described by his cat as follows: "That thing is My man; … He is very strong because he eats a lot; he is an All-eater. ('What are you eating? Give it to Me!') He is not beautiful, for he has no fur. He hasn't enough spittle, so he has to wash himself with water."

Pulcinella, the cat of the Italian composer **Domenico Scarlatti** (1685–1757). The feline loved to walk on the keys of the clavichord, and thus apparently inspiring Scarlatti's Fugue in G minor—commonly known as the *Cat's Fugue*.

Puss in Boots is the inventive leading character of a popular fable first transcribed by the Italian **Giovanni Francesco Straparola** (1480–1557). The feline would become famous in the French version, "Le Chat Botté" (1697), of **Charles Perrault** (1628–1703) and as "Der gestiefelte Kater" in the *Grimm's Fairy Tales* (1812) published by the Grimm brothers (Jakob, 1785–1863; Wilhelm, 1786–1859). Puss in Boots has recently starred on the silver screen, in Chris Miller's 2011 spinoff of *Shrek 2* (DreamWorks Animation), in which the outlaw cat has the voice of Antonio Banderas.

for *Persian*

The descendant of long-haired cats from Persia (modern-day Iran), and perhaps even depicted by the ancient Egyptians, this breed has been greatly admired since the first competitive cat show was held at the Crystal Palace, London, in 1871. Since then, thanks to its chubby muzzle, round eyes and peaceful disposition, it has become the most widespread breed in the United States.

Coat: long-haired and dense, requires daily grooming; more than 180 colors and patterns, including solid, silver and golden, shaded and smoke, tabby, particolor and bicolor

Temperament: calm, gentle; loves peace and quiet, and a regular routine; strictly a housecat

Praline🐾

The kitty curled up in her compassionate arms with a trusting and blissful air that touched Adele.

…

"Mom! Look at this poor little pussy cat! I saved her life, Mom! I bought her from some bad kids who were torturing her and wanted to skin her alive. Yes, Mom. That's what they said. I did the right thing buying her, Mom. Right? You're not mad, Mom, are you? That I brought this poor little guest here? I couldn't leave her with her torturers, right, Mom?"

Adele's mother smiled at the miserable creature.

"Your protégé is not pretty," she said, "and, dear child, I fear she will be very rude and Jannette will end up complaining."

"But I'll teach her to be polite, Mom!" Adele exclaimed. "I'm sure she's really bright. Look! Doesn't she have an expressive face? It almost seems like she understands what we're saying."

"Yes ma'am," said Jannette, hands on her hips and shaking her head. "Would you believe that Miss Adele paid her twenty cents to get this little monster? I wonder if she wouldn't have preferred a few ounces of those wonderful pink pralines I love so much."

"Sigh!" said Adele, thinking about the candy she had sacrificed; tomorrow the pralines would already have been eaten, but she'd still have my cat… "What about calling her 'Praline'? Mom, what do you think? Isn't that a lovely name?"

"Wonderful, sweetheart!"

"Then it's decided!" exclaimed Adele. "Her name is Praline! Did you hear that, kitty? Your name is Praline: Pay close attention and answer me whenever I call you!"

"Mi-a-ow!" responded the cat.

Henriette Pravaz and Jules Girardet (Illus.), *Histoire de Praline*,
Paris: Librairie C. Delagrave, 1890, pp. 11–12.

🐾The lovely white kitten with one green eye and one blue, rescued by Adele and her faithful companion in her adventures, along with the little dog Froufrou and the hen Coqueriquette.

Quaker, the second Station Cat at the former Kirkby Stephen East Railway Station, Cumbria, which is currently undergoing restoration. She was preceded by "**Rabbit** the Station Cat." A black-and-white cat, Quaker's name was inspired by the moniker of the local Darlington Football Club, nicknamed "the Quakers," due to its black-and-white livery and the team's black-and-white home colors.

Tom Quartz (1), the cat of "grave and simple **Dick Baker**," an expert gold miner (the cat more so than Baker) in *Roughing It* (1872), **Mark Twain**'s semiautobiographical travel volume. In Chapter LXI, Baker mourns the "wonderful cat he used to own," describing it "with the air of a man who believed in his secret heart that there was something human about it—may be even supernatural": "Gentlemen, I used to have a cat here, by the name of Tom Quartz, which you'd a took an interest in I reckon—most any body would. I had him here eight year—and he was the remarkablest cat I ever ever see. He was a large gray one of the Tom specie, an' he had more hard, natchral sense than any man in this camp—'n' a power of dignity—he wouldn't let the Gov'ner of Californy be familiar with him. He never ketched a rat in his life—'peared to be above it. He never cared for nothing but mining. He knowed more about mining, that cat did, than any man I ever, ever see. You couldn't tell him noth'n 'bout placer diggin's—'n' as for pocket mining, why he was just born for it."

Tom Quartz (2), the naughty cat of the **Theodore Roosevelt** (1858–1919), president of the United States, hunter, naturalist, writer and orator, who recounted one of this feline's escapades in a letter to his son Kermit (January 6, 1903). "Another evening, the next Speaker of the House, Mr. Cannon, an exceedingly solemn, elderly gentleman with chin whiskers, who certainly does not look to be of playful nature, came to call upon me. He is a great friend of mine, and we sat talking over what our policies for the session should be until about eleven o'clock; and when he went away I accompanied him to the head of the stairs. He had gone about halfway down when Tom Quartz strolled by, his tail erect and very fluffy. He spied Mr. Cannon going down the stairs, jumped to the conclusion that he was a playmate escaping, and raced after him, suddenly grasping him by the leg the way he does Archie and Quentin when they play hide and seek with him; then loosening his hold he tore downstairs ahead of Mr. Cannon, who eyed him with iron calm and not one particle of surprise."
See also Slippers (p. 86)

Queen Cat, the black cat of **Nina Simone** (1933–2003), American queen of jazz. In 1987, the song *My Baby Just Cares for Me* rocketed to number one in the world's top ten, thanks, at least in part, to an Aardman Animations video, directed by Peter Lord, in which a black cat representing Simone sings in a nightclub before the gaze of an ardent admirer, a white cat.

Queenie, the stray that decided to spend Christmas 1998 with the British royal family at Sandringham, their country retreat in Norfolk.

QuiQui, the cats of the French painter **Narcisse Berchère** (1819–91), transformed into a panther in a drawing by his friend and fellow artist **Gustave Moreau** (1826–98).

for *quitt ('cat' in Arabic)*

Also, *qattus* (in Maltese). "The phrase 'domestic cat' is an oxymoron" (George F. Will)
—this quote is particularly apt for describing the Bengal, a cross between a domestic cat
and an Asian leopard cat, as noted above. But even the most tranquil housecat owes its adaptability and,
thus, survival to its feral intelligence. Although their brain is quite small, it seems that, regardless of the eternal
controversy about the "superior intelligence" of dogs, cats have twice as many neurons—and a formidable memory.

Q for IQ

Cat haiku:

My brain: walnut-sized.
Yours: largest among the primates.
Yet, who leaves for work?

(Anon, n.d.)

Rufus lay in his bean-bag, and purred every time he thought of it, and he watched us, and watched the two other cats watching him. Then he made a new move. By now we knew he never did anything without very good reason, that first he worked things out, and then acted.

[…]

Rufus made me think about the different kinds of cat intelligence. Before that I had recognized that cats had different temperaments. His is the intelligence of the survivor. Charles has the scientific intelligence, curious about everything, human affairs, the people who come to the house, and, in particular, our gadgets. […] When he was a kitten, before he gave up, he used to stop a turning record with a paw … release it … stop it again … look at us, miaow an enquiry. He would walk to the back of the radio set to find out if he could see what he heard, go behind the television set, turn over a tape recorder with his paw, sniff at it, miaow, What is this? He is the talkative cat. He talks you down the stairs and out of the house, talks you in again and up the stairs, he comments on everything that happens. When he comes in from the garden you can hear him from the top of the house. 'Here I am at last,' he cries, 'Charles the adorable, and how you must have missed me! Just imagine what has happened to me, you'll never believe it…' Into the room you are sitting in he comes, and stands in the doorway, his head slightly on one side, and waits for you to admire him. 'Am I not the prettiest cat in this house?' he demands, vibrating all over. Winsome, that's the word for Charles.

The General has his intuitive intelligence, knowing what you are thinking, and what you are going to do next. He is not interested in science, how things work; he does not bother to impress you with his looks. He talks when he has something to say and only when he is alone with you. 'Ah,' he says, finding that the other cats are elsewhere, 'so we are alone at last.' And he permits a duet of mutual admiration. When I come back from somewhere he rushes from the end of the garden crying out 'There you are, I've missed you! How could you go away and leave me for so long?' He leaps into my arms, licks my face and, unable to contain his joy, rushes all over the house like a kitten. Then he returns to being his grave and dignified self.

Doris Lessing, "Rufus", in *Particularly Cats… and Rufus*, New York: Knopf, 1991.

Rabbi Ben Ezra ("Rab") *see Waif*

Racan *see Félimare*

Raton, the cat who pulls roasted chestnuts from the embers for Bertrand the monkey in the fable "The Monkey and the Cat" (*Fables Choisies*, 1679) by **Jean de La Fontaine** (1621–95), and also the name of the feline celebrated in the verses of the French poet **Jacques Delille** (1738–1813).

Rodilardus ("Old Rodilard"), the "dread rat-eater" in the fable *The Council Held by the Rats* by **Jean de La Fontaine** (1621–95).

Rhubarb, the furry protagonist of the 1951 film by the same name directed by Arthur Lubin, in which he is played by **Orangey**, who thus won his first PATSY (Picture Animal Top Star of the Year) Award.
See also Orangey

Rubis-sur-l'Ongle, *see Félimare*

Ruffy and Rocky, *see Snowbell*

Rufus, the arthritic orange stray who made his way into the home and heart of the Nobel Laureate in Literature **Doris Lessing** (b. 1919), author of *Particularly Cats* (including the essay "Rufus the Survivor") (1993). (*See* p. 78)
See also Charles and El Magnifico

Raminagrobis is the name of the "prince of cats" in French folklore. In the fable "The Cat, the Weasel and the Little Rabbit" by **Jean de La Fontaine** (1621–95), he is a duplicitous "hermit cat … a saintly mouser, sleek and fat"; he is also the merciless "veteran cat" in "The Old Cat and the Young Mouse."

Ratonne, an elderly black-and-white stray that the French novelist **Pierre Loti** (1850–1923) took in and cared for. In fact, he was the only one who could cuddle the cat.
See also Belaud (2) and Le Chat

Rome, one of the cats of the French art historian **Pierre Rosenberg** (b. 1936), author—with Elisabeth Foucart-Walter—of *The Painted Cat: The Cat in Western Painting from the Fifteenth to the Twentieth Century* (1987), and former director of the Musée du Louvre.

Red, the cat who—unlike Rhubarb—really *did* inherit a fortune. His owner, **David Harper**, left him assets worth almost a million dollars, to be administrated by the United Church of Canada, which now provides for his care and well-being.

Rudimace, the tabby of the English poet **W. H. Auden** (1907–73), who observed: "Cats can be very funny, and have the oddest ways of showing they're glad to see you. Rudimace always peed in our shoes."

Rumple, *see Jake*

Ringo de Balmalon, later renamed "Gris-Gris," the loyal Chartreux of the French general **Charles De Gaulle** (1890–1970).

Ripley, the unsurprising name of one of the Siamese cats of psychological thriller writer **Patricia Highsmith** (1921–95), author of *The Talented Mr. Ripley* (1955) (the first in a series of five) as well as various cat-themed tales.

Raminou, the ginger tabby portrayed a number of times by the French painter **Suzanne Valadon** (1865–1938), herself the muse of Degas, Renoir and Toulouse-Lautrec. Raminou accompanied Valadon amongst the artistic community of Montmartre in Paris, and appears in paintings by Renoir and Steinlen.

Rosa Luxemburg, cat of the Russian revolutionary **Vladimir Lenin** (1870–1924), at least according to apocryphal accounts. What is certain is that "Mimi," the cat of the revolutionary socialist **Rosa Luxembourg** (1871–1919), "impressed Lenin tremendously; he said that only in Siberia had he seen such a magnificent creature, that she was... a majestic cat. She also flirted with him, rolled on her back and behaved enticingly, but, when he tried to approach her, she whacked him with a paw and snarled like a tiger."

Rumpelstilzchen, *see Hurlyburlybuss*

Rupi, the cat of **Ian Anderson** (b. 1947), lead vocalist and founder of the British rock band Jethro Tull. Rupi inspired the title song—and features on the front cover—of Anderson's 2003 solo album *Rupi's Dance*.

for *Ragdoll*

First bred in California in 1960, this cat was given its name because it goes completely floppy and limp when picked up. Adult cats are some of the largest of the registered domestic breeds.
Coat: medium-long, longer on the ruff and fluffy tail
Temperament: extremely docile, the most gentle, well-behaved and affectionate of cats (indeed, it is overly trusting, so it is advisable not to let a Ragdoll out); loves water and bathtubs

Rybolov✥

Several tom-cats that found a home in [the Russian composer] Borodin's apartment paraded across the dinner-table, sticking their noses into plates, unceremoniously leaping to the diner's back. These tom-cats basked in Yekatyerina Sergeyevna's protection; various details of their biography were related. One tabby was called Rybolov (Fisherman), because, in the winter, he contrived to catch small fish with his paw through the ice-holes; the other was called Dlinyenki (Longy) and he was in the habit of fetching homeless kittens by the neck to Borodin's apartment; these the Borodins would harbor, later finding homes for them.

Nikolay Rimsky-Korsakov, Nadezhda Nikolaevna Rimskaia-Korsakova *et al.* (eds.),
My Musical Life, New York, NY: A. A. Knopf, 1923, p. 164.

✥ One of the cats of the eminent Russian chemist and composer Aleksandr Porfir'evič Borodin (1833–87).

Saha, the Chartreux cat with which **Alain** has hopelessly fallen in love, and of which his wife Camille is insanely jealous. It isn't hard to guess who will ultimately win in **Colette**'s novel, *La Chatte* (1933). "At the bottom of the hole left by the yew, Saha smelled a mole and the image—if not the odor—went to her head. For a whole minute, lost in her frenzy, she dug like a fox terrier, curled up like an armadillo, jumped on all fours like a toad, hid a ball of soil between her thighs like a field mouse does with the egg it has stolen, and emerged from the hole, performing a series of acrobatic feats and ending up sitting on the grass, cool and collected, controlling her breathing."

Sappho, one of the cats often portrayed by the Japanese painter and printmaker **Léonard Tsuguharu Foujita** (1886–1968).

Selima, the unfortunate tortoiseshell cat of **Horace Walpole** (1717–97) that inspired Thomas Gray to write *Ode on the Death of a Favourite Cat, Drowned in a Tub of Gold Fishes* (1748).
See also Harold

Shirley, one of the 11 cats of the late British singer and songwriter **Amy Winehouse** (1983–2011).

Snowdrop, *see Dinah*

Socks, the black cat with white paws that was a White House denizen during the presidency of **Bill Clinton** (b. 1946) and thus was also known as "First Cat."

Spithead, cat of the English scientist **Sir Isaac Newton** (1642–1727). It is thanks to him that the father of the law of universal gravitation invented the cat-door—in order not be disturbed by Spithead's comings and goings from his study.

Stanley, the orange tabby in "Miss Paisley's Cat," an episode that aired in 1957 as part of the television series *Alfred Hitchcock Presents*, Hitchcock introduced the episode as follows: "Oh, good evening. The leading man in tonight's saga is an alley cat. He must be fed before each performance. It keeps him from eating the actors. Tonight he's having finely chopped mice burger. Naturally, we used nothing but contented mice. For two weeks, they were fed nothing but tranquilizers. Now, just as soon as I can feed our star, you should see our story: 'Miss Paisley's Cat'…"

Satan, the black cat with incandescent eyes of **Judith Gautier** (1845–1917), French author, Oriental scholar and one of Théophile Gautier's two daughters. Before they could take a seat, Sunday guests had to present their gifts to Satan and undergo his critical inspection.
See also Iblis

Sneaky Pie Brown, the ginger tabby who, with **Rita Mae Brown** (b. 1944), "coauthored" the series of mysteries about the postmistress **Mary Minor Haristeen** and her cats, Mrs. **Murphy** (the "tiger cat"), Pewter (a chubby gray kitten) and the corgi Tee Tucker, from *Wish You Were Here* (1990) to *A Nose for Justice* (2012).

Solomon, the white Turkish Angora who played the placid cat stroked by James Bond's bitter enemy **Ernst Stavro Blofeld**, head of SPECTRE. The feline also appeared in Stanley Kubrick's film *A Clockwork Orange* (1971).

Spot, the cat of the android **Data** (played by Brent Spiner) in the television series *Star Trek: The Next Generation*. Spot was initially played by a Somali cat called Monster, but in later episodes was replaced by an orange tabby.

Sprite, the friendly and intelligent gray tabby of cartoonist **Bill Watterson** (b. 1958) that inspired the character of Hobbes, the toy tiger in the comic strip *Calvin and Hobbes*.

Suzy, cat of **Louise Brooks** (1906–85), the American dancer and star of silent films.

Salem Saberhagen, **Sabrina**'s talking black cat in the American television series *Sabrina the Teenage Witch* (1996–2003).

Salt and Pepper, the two cats—one white, the other black—of the Beatle **John Lennon** (1940–80) and **Yoko Ono** (b. 1933).

Scheherazade, the "bowl of a cat" of American writer and photographer **Carl Van Vechten** (1880–1964). "This cat enjoyed a pleasant habit of sleeping in a great yellow salad bowl, curled up with her tail protruding over the brim."
See also Ariel, Feathers

Shuang-mei ("Eyebrows of Frost"), the blue cat with white eyebrows who was the favorite of the eleventh emperor of the Ming Dynasty of China, **Jiajing**, born Zhu Houcong (1507–67).

Sam, the name of most of the cats of the American artist **Andy Warhol** (1928–87), and certainly that of 16 of the multicolor cats in the privately printed collection of lithographs entitled *25 Cats Name* [sic] *Sam and One Blue Pussy* (1954).
See also Hester

Si, *see Am*

Siam, the name of the first Siamese cat to tread upon American soil. He was so named by the then U.S. president **Rutherford B. Hayes** (1822–93), who received him as a gift in 1877.

Snowbell, the white Persian at the Little household in E. B. White's book *Stuart Little* (1945), made into a movie in 1999 (Columbia Pictures). In *Stuart Little 2* (2002), four cats were used to play the role: **Ruffy** and **Tuffy** (as "stunt cats"), **Rocky** (for pursuits) and **Lucky Prince** (close-ups).

Sylvester, the black-and-white "puddy tat" with an unmistakable lisp, created by Warner Bros. in 1945 and originally called "**Thomas**." In the 1947 animation *Tweetie Pie*, Tweety Bird (also known as "Tweety Pie") first squawked his signature refrain: "I tawt I taw a puddy tat!"

Syn Cat, the intrepid Siamese that debuted in cinema in the role of agent "D.C." in the movie *That Darn Cat* (1965). Despite Syn Cat's immediate fame, acknowledged by a PATSY Award, he continued to be a docile cat with his paws firmly planted on the ground—unlike his colleagues (*see* "**Orangey**").

for *Siamese*

This cat boasts noble origins. It is thought that, originally, only members of the royal family of Siam (modern-day Thailand) could own them and give them as gifts, but in the late nineteenth century the breed came to be known around the world, and was first certified in 1934.

Coat: short-haired; kittens are generally white at birth, but develop points coloration on the extremities of their body (face, ears, feet, tail) in the first few months; adult Siamese living in warm climates often have lighter coats than those living in cold climates

Temperament: arguably the most intelligent and vocal of the domestic cats, it makes itself understood and gets what it wants

Slippers ❖

Doubtless there never was, and never will be, another cat that has had respectful homage paid it by representatives of so many great and little powers of the world. But such was the experience of "Slippers" in the year of grace 1906. Slippers was the name of the White House cat. Gray in color, and having six toes, it was this unusual foot-furnishing that earned his name. Perhaps because of a surplusage of dogs in this generation; perhaps because of an inbred Americanism that makes him assert his independence as a democratic cat, even in the White House under a Republican administration, and long to perch upon the back fence with others of his kind; perhaps just because he was a cat—Slippers had a habit of absenting himself from his post for days and weeks at time. But, however long he stayed away, he never failed to turn up just before a big diplomatic dinner. How he knew, I cannot tell. No one can. But that he did know is certain. Anyone who kept a steady eye on the White House did not need to be told by the newspapers when a State dinner was impending. When he saw Slippers sunning himself on the front steps, that was enough. The cards were out.

Thus came about the historic occasion I hinted at. The dinner was over, and the President, with the wife of a distinguished Ambassador on his arm, led the procession from the state-dining room along the wide corridor to the East Room at the other end of the building: Ambassadors and the plenipotentiaries and ministers following, according to their rank in the official world, all chattering happily with their ladies, seeing no cloud on the diplomatic horizon; when all of a sudden the glittering procession came to a halt. There, on the rug, in the exact middle of the corridor, lay Slippers, stretched out at full length and blinking lazily at the fine show which no doubt he thought got up especially to do him honor. The President saw him in time to avoid treading on him and stopped. His first impulse was to pick Slippers up, but a little shiver of his lady and a half suppressed exclamation, as he bent over the cat, warned him that she did not like cats, or was afraid, and for a moment he was perplexed. Slippers, perceiving the attention bestowed on him, rolled luxuriously on the rug, purring his delight. No thought of moving out of the path was in his mind. There was but one thing to do, and the man who found the way to make peace between Russia and Japan did it quickly. With an amused bow, as if in apology to the Ambassadress, he escorted her round Slippers, and kept his way toward the East Room. Whereupon the representatives of Great Britain, and of France, of Germany, and Italy, and all the Empires and of the little kingdoms, followed suit, paying their respects to Slippers quite as effectually as if the warship of their nations had thundered out a salute at an expenditure of powder that would have kept a poor man comfortable for years, and certainly have scared even a White House cat almost to death.

JACOB A. RIIS, "Slippers, the White House cat," in *St. Nicholas Magazine*, January, 1908.

❖The White House cat that, after almost sparking a
diplomatic incident, became the most revered feline in
the world, as well as being the personal cat of President
Theodore Roosevelt (1858–1919). In fact, fearing that, after
the episode described here, the White House staff would
"deal with" Slippers, the President excused himself for a
moment and went back to find the cat, immediately taking
it to the First Lady so she could stroke him and admire his
undertaking.

Tabby (1), the cat of Abraham Lincoln (1809–65), sixteenth president of the United States.

Tango, the marmalade neutered male cat (though referred to as "she") of **Sir Winston Churchill** (1874–1965). Tango features in a Churchill family portrait painted by Sir William Nicholson.

See also Jock and Nelson

Ted NudeGent, the disconsolate Sphynx that played **Mr. Bigglesworth**, the cat of **Dr. Evil**, in *Austin Powers: International Man of Mystery* (1997).

Tinker Toy, the smallest cat ever, according to *The Guinness Book of World Records*. A male blue point Himalayan-Persian, he was just 2.75 inches (7 cm) tall and 7.5 inches (19 cm) long.

Tobermory, "a 'Beyond-cat' of extraordinary intelligence" whom Mr. Cornelius Appin taught to speak, sowing panic among the guests of Lady Blemley, when, with great aplomb and utter indiscretion, he reveals all the party's goings-on, in *The Chronicles of Clovis* (1911), a volume of short stories by the **Saki** (1870–1916).

Topper, the black-and-white cat who starred in Jane Campion's film *Bright Star* (2009), based on the final years in the life of the poet John Keats. The cat steals the show every time he appears on screen.

Tabby (2), **Tavy**, **Tittlebat**, **Tommy** and **Toozle**, *see Octavius*

Tao, the Siamese cat who, with the Labrador retriever Luath and the bull terrier Bodger, crossed Canada in the 1963 Walt Disney film and in the original novel *The Incredible Journey* (1961) by **Sheila Burnford** (1918–84).

Thisbé, *see Pyram*

Thomas O'Malley, the alley cat who falls in love with the elegant **Duchess** and help her and her kittens: **Toulouse**, the orange one with a penchant for painting, **Marie**, white like her mother, and **Berlioz** in the animated Walt Disney Productions film *Aristocats* (1970).

Mr. Tinkles, the white Persian with delusions of grandeur in the 2001 film *Cats and Dogs*. His plan? To render all humans allergic to dogs in order that cats might conquer the world (as if they haven't already done so…).

Tom (1), the first cat to make the name "Tom the Cat" famous ("tomcat" refers specifically to male cats), appeared in the children's book *The Life and Adventures of a Cat*, published in 1760.

Toto, the cat who, in 1944, apparently prompted people to evacuate just prior to the eruption of Mount Vesuvius, Italy.

Thomasina, the cat convinced she was an Egyptian deity in the 1957 novel by **Paul Gallico** (1897–1976) entitled *Thomasina: The Cat Who Thought She Was God*, later made into the Walt Disney film *The Three Lives of Thomasina* in 1964.

Tom (2), the cat who, since the 1940s, has chased the mouse Jerry in the cartoon films bearing their names created by William Hanna and Joseph Barbera for Metro-Goldwyn-Mayer.

Toufou, the cat of **René Barjavel** (1911–85), the French journalist and science fiction writer.

Taki, the "secretary" (a magnificent black Persian) of **Raymond Chandler** (1888–1959), creator of the private detective Philip Marlowe. Her assistance involved sitting on the proofs as Chandler tried to correct them. She is also known for writing a letter to another cat: "Come around sometime when your face is clean and we shall discuss the state of the world, the foolishness of humans, the prevalence of horsemeat, although we prefer the tenderloin side of a porterhouse, and our common difficulty in getting doors opened at the right time and meals served at more frequent intervals. I have got my staff up to five a day, but there is still room for improvement."

Tibert ("Tybalt"), the cat who completes in cunning with Reynard the fox in medieval European folklore, as depicted in *Le Roman de Renart*, an Old French collection of eleventh- and twelfth-century versions of the original fables.

Tiger, the cat of **Emily Brontë** (1818–48) who played at her feet while she was writing *Wuthering Heights* (1847). He probably also played with the other cats mentioned in Emily's letters and the diaries of her younger sister Anne: **Tabby** (3), **Martha Brown**, **Flossey** and **Keeper**.

Tom Kitten, the cat of **Caroline** (b. 1957), daughter of former U.S. president John F. Kennedy (1917–63). He was the first feline resident in the White House after **Slippers** (*see* p. 86).

Tonto, the orange cat and travel companion on the coast-to-coast journey undertaken by **Harry** (played by Art Carney) in the road movie *Harry and Tonto* (1974).

Tweedledum and **Tweedledee**, the "two handsome brothers, christened stupidly" by Canon **Henry Parry Liddon** (1829–1890), the Anglican scholar and writer.

Tyke, the cat of the American writer **Jack Kérouac** (1922–69). This is how the author of *On the Road* (1957) recalled him in *Big Sur* (1962): "I loved Tyke with all my heart, he was my baby who as a kitten just slept in the palm of my hand and with his little head hanging down, or just purring for hours, just as long as I held him that way, walking or sitting – He was like a floppy fur wrap around my wrist, I just twist him around my wrist or drape him and he just purred and purred and even when he got big I still held him that way, I could even hold that big cat in both hands with my arms outstretched right over my head and he'd just purr, he had complete confidence in me."

for *Tonkinese*

Bred in Canada in the 1960s by crossing a Burmese and a Siamese, the breed was formally recognized in 1979. The Tonkinese is widely admired for its characteristic aquamarine eyes, although this is not the only eye color the breed can have.

Coat: short-haired; recognized patterns encompass solid (from the sepia Burmese), pointed (Siamese pattern) and mink (unique to the Tonkinese)

Temperament: outgoing and sociable; craves attention and company

Tittums ❀

I made sure that he had gone to the yard, but when I looked into the passage ten minutes later he [Gustavus Adolphus, the dog] was sitting at the top of the stairs. I ordered him down at once, but he only barked and jumped about, so I went to see what was the matter.

It was Tittums. She was sitting on the top stair but one and wouldn't let him pass.

Tittums is our kitten. She is about the size of a penny roll. Her back was up and she was swearing like a medical student.

She does swear fearfully. I do a little that way myself sometimes, but I am a mere amateur compared with her. … Swearing relieves the feeling—that is swearing does. I explained this to my aunt on one occasion, but it didn't answer with her. She said I had no business to have such feelings.

That is what I told Tittums. I told her she ought to be ashamed of herself, brought up in a Christian family as she was, too. I don't so much mind hearing an old cat swear, but I can't bear to see a mere kitten give way to it. It seems sad in one so young.

I put Tittums in my pocket and returned to my desk. I forgot her for the moment, and when I looked I found that she had squirmed out of my pocket on to the table and was trying to swallow the pen; then she put her leg into the ink-pot and upset it; then she licked her leg; then she swore again—at me this time.

JEROME K. JEROME, "On Cats and Dogs," in
Idle Thoughts of an Idle Fellow, New York: Scribner & Welford, 1886.

❀The irascible, lively cat of the English satirist Jerome K.
Jerome (1859–1927), which, not content with terrifying
the huge Gustavus Adolphus, also scratches the nose of the
imprudent Tim, a young fox terrier with "the airs of a
gray-headed Scotch collie."

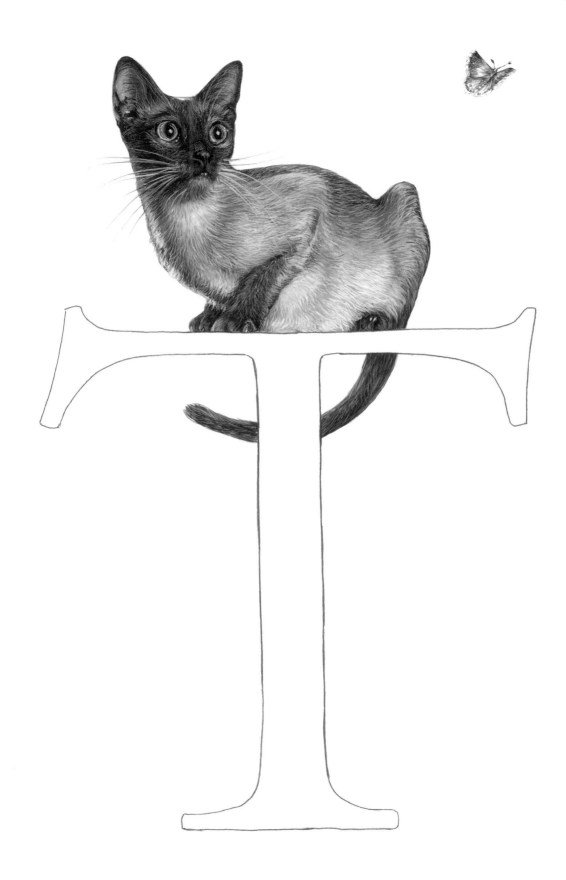

U-Boat, mascot of the British corvette HMS *Snowflake*. A member of the ship's complement (he had his own hammock and lifejacket), U-Boat would disembark at each port of call yet knew exactly when to return aboard. Only once did he fail to appear on time. Part of the crew was considering mutiny, as it bad luck to leave without the ship's cat, and the corvette had already cast off moorings when, suddenly, a gray shadow appeared on the dock, took a huge leap… and, luckily, landed safely on the bridge.

Uli, one of the six cats—the others are Angel, Micia, Nerone, Annibale and Marchesini—owned by the Italian designer **Giorgio Armani** (b. 1934), who naturally appreciates feline elegance.

Ulla, Ulric's sister (*see* below). He constantly steals her food, which may be why she has kept her slim-line figure.

Ulric, the overweight Norwegian from Dorset who, at nearly 28 pounds, is more than twice his ideal weight, and is the fattest finalist in Pet Fit Club, a weight-loss competition promoted by the British animal charity PDSA.

Uncle Wolfe, one of the 54 cats of Ernest Hemingway (1899–1961). Though he was Boise's son, he didn't inherit any of his father's adventurousness, and was instead quite shy and conservative (hating anything new). Because of his long gray coat, inherited from his mother, the Persian Princessa, he was also referred to as "Snow Leopard." Uncle Wolfe appears in Hemingway's posthumously published novel *Islands in the Stream* (1970). *See also Boise, Izzy the Cat and Sir Winston Churchill*

Unsinkable Sam, *see Oscar (1)*

for *Usual (Abyssinian)*

"Usual" is the name of the original coat color of the Abyssinian. It also known as "ruddy," because of its reddish-brown base, or "hare," because of it resemblance to the coat of this animal. It features a black "ticking" coloration, and the feet and the backs of the hind legs are black, too. One of the oldest breeds in the world, the Abyssinian boasts forbearers that were portrayed by the ancient Egyptians, and even now, centuries later, it has maintained the wild appearance of its ancient ancestor *Felis silvestris lybica*.

Coat: short-haired, dense, with visible "ticking" (each hair has a base color broken up by darker bands and ending with a dark tip)

Temperament: affectionate but irrepressible (with kittens, it is advisable to stow knick-knacks in a safe place)

Unique

"There are no ordinary cats."
(Colette, 1949)

Colette, *Chats de Colette*, Paris: Albin Michel, 1949.

Vaino, the 12-year-old Finnish cat who, after getting lost on vacation in a camper with his owners, **Ari** and **Katarina Salo**, managed to find his way home—covering 800 kilometers in 130 days.

Vaske, the white and tiger-striped cat of Vassily Kandinsky (1866–1944), the Russian painter who launched abstract art.

Verdi and **Vivaldi**, both two Himalayans, are two of many cats, dogs, canaries, chickens, chinchillas and other pets of the American television personality and animal lover **Martha Stewart** (b. 1941).

Victor, whose official name was **Champion Laurel King**, son of the **Laurel Queen**, was owned by **Charles Henry Lane**, a nineteenth-century cat breeder and one of the first authors of a manual on cat breeds. Victor won competitions through behaving like a "gentlecat," but would instantly turn into a fury as soon as he sensed another cat was about to invade his territory.
See also Laurel Queen and Yellow Boy

Vincent and **Wart**, the two cats of **Robert Goulet** (1933–2007) who accompanied the American singer and actor on tour for the musical *Camelot*, which opened in Toronto, Canada, in 1960.

Miss Vixen, the black cat transformed from "yacht cat" to "war cat" when the U.S. Navy purchased the yacht *Orion* (renamed USS *Vixen*) for military use in the Caribbean from 1941 to 1946.

Valeriano Weyler and **Enrique DeLome**, the two Angoras of former U.S. president **William McKinley** (1843–1901).

Venus, the cat of the Welsh poet **William Henry Davies** (1871–1940), whose collection *The Song of Life* (1920) includes a poem called "The Cat."

Vesper, the devout black cat that, in 1996, entered the church of St. Mary of the Angels in Hollywood. In the Catholic and Anglican tradition, Vespers is another name for evening prayer; "Vesper" the cat attends Mass and has apparently even taken her vows, going from "novice" to "mother superior."

Victoria, the White Cat who opens the Jellicle Ball in the stage musical *Cats* by Andrew Lloyd Webber, based on T. S. Eliot's *Old Possum's Book of Practical Cats* (1939), and performed in more than 250 cities around the world, following the 1981 premiere at the New London Theatre.
See also Asparagus, Jellylorum and Wiscus

Virgil, *see Ovid (p. 70)*

Varjak Paw, the leading character in the eponymous 2003 children's book by **S. F. Said** (b. 1967). He is a Mesopotamian Blue (a fictional breed) that has never left the house on the hill where he lives with his family. But, one day, the arrival of a mysterious Gentleman and the stories of his grandfather, **Elder Paw**, about "The Way," a secret form of cat martial arts practiced by his forebearer **Jalal**, inspire him to venture into the city.
See also Julius

Vulpi, the golden Persian of the German-born writer **Carmen Sylva** (Elisabeth of Wied, queen of Romania) (1843–1916).
See also Frätzibutzi and Püffchen

for *Turkish Van*

This breed is thought to have originated in the Lake Van region of southeastern Turkey. In 1955, a breeding pair of Vans was captured and brought back to England. The breed was recognized in 1969 (GCCF). It has still not lost its habit of hunting by diving into water if necessary.
Coat: medium-long, white, with a golden red tail and ears
Temperament: strong personality, courageous, playful, with a melodious meow

Vashka ♣

Talk about a princely diet! This is a recipe for the food that was to be served to the Tsar's cat.

1. Lightly marinate two cups of Belgian caviar and two cups of gold caviar in top-quality Champagne.
2. Add the finely minced meat of an edible rodent imported from France.
3. Stir the yolk of a pheasant egg and a spoonful of hare's blood into warm butter.
4. Cook over low heat with cream.
5. Once cooled, sprinkle with chopped chervil and Sukhumi cheese.

On warm days—again, as per the Tsar's instructions—a splash of dry Champagne had to be added.

♣The Russian Blue favored by Tsar Nicholas I (1796–1855),
which was kidnapped twice by the emperor's adversaries,
but found both times.

Wabbit, the gray cat of the British actress **Kate Beckinsale** (b. 1973). In 2006, the star of *Underworld Evolution* had to retrieve him from the roof of a neighbor's house in Santa Monica, California. In 2012, he disappeared again and so Kate hired a pair of "pet detectives," who "found" a way to clog Kate's bathroom and then, a little later, presented her an envelope of "evidence"—coyote excrement (to be analyzed for traces of Wabbit...).

Wallad, the Syrian cat of a New Zealand soldier, **George McAllister**. Handsome but "incurably lazy," Wallad is recorded as hunting his first (and, in all likelihood, last) mouse on October 12, 1942, thanks to the "help and encouragement of a noisy mob of troopers." However, as soon as he had captured his prey, Wallad promptly went to sleep.

Willie, cat of **George Burns** (1896–1996), the American actor and comedian. The cat was dubbed Willie "because, when you told the cat what to do, it was always a question of 'will he or won't he.'"

Willy, a cat with a passion for gardening gloves. When spring arrives in Pelham, New York, **Jeannine Goche** puts up a sign in front of her house: "Our cat is a glove snatcher. Please take these if yours."

Wiscus, one of the many cats of **T. S. Eliot** (1888–1965), the English poet, playwright and Nobel Laureate. Along with Noilly Prat, Pattipaws, George Pushdragon and Tantomile, he almost certainly helped to inspire the fabulous felines featured in *Old Possum's Book of Practical Cats* (1939).
See also Asparagus, Jellylorym and Victoria

Wong Wong, a Havana Brown who, along with fellow artist **Lu Lu** (a Seal Lynx), created about a dozen paintings. Their most famous work, *Wonglu*, was auctioned in 1993 for U.S.$19,000.

Wart, *see Vincent*

Wellington, the troubling black cat of the orphan **Lucy** in the second segment of the horror film *The Uncanny* (1977), which featured the strapline "Cats aren't always cute and cuddly"...

Waif, one of the many cats of **Walter Herries Pollock** (1850–1926), the English journalist and author of *Animals That Have Owned Us* (1904): "The cat thinks the world was made for him." And how right he was! Pollock's cats included Catkin, Count ("Tommie") Lestrange, Dabado, Pucky, Rabbi Ben Ezra ("Rab"), Toots and Tottie.

Mr. Peter Wells, cat of **H. G. Wells** (1866–1946), who wrote *The War of the Worlds* (1898). Peter disliked prolix and noisy guests, and would make his displeasure known by ostentatiously leaving the room.

Wilberforce worked tirelessly as a mouser at 10 Downing Street from 1973 to 1987, serving under four British prime ministers. According to Margaret Thatcher's press secretary, the Iron Lady once bought Wilberforce "a tin of sardines in a Moscow supermarket."
See also Humphrey

White Heather, the beloved chubby Angora of **Queen Victoria** (1819–1901), who survived the longest reigning British monarch and was passed on to her son Edward VII.

Windy, cat and co-pilot of RAF commander **Guy Gibson** (1918–44) in his missions during World War II.

Sir Winston Churchill, one of the 54 felines of the American writer **Ernest Hemingway** (1899–1961). Sulky and solitary, he spurned milk and cream, but loved meat and fish (although apparently only if marinated in alcoholic beverages).
See also Boise, Izzy the Cat and Uncle Wolfe

Fred Wunpound, mouser and mascot, who retired in 1975 after 250,000 miles and eight years of service as Leading Seacat aboard the British Royal Navy survey vessel HMS *Hecate*.

for *Black & White*

Both pure white and pure black coat colors are the result of genetic combinations. White is a dominant gene that masks every other color, and is sometimes associated with deafness in cats. Black is a spontaneous genetic mutation—the same one that transformed the leopard into a panther. The quintessential black cat, bred in 1958 for the specific purpose of obtaining a miniature panther, is the American Bombay, while the odd-eyed Turkish Angora is the oldest snow-white cat. A combination of the two colors can be found in both pedigree and non-pedigree cats; referred to as "tuxedo cats" in the United States, the best known examples are perhaps the *Looney Tunes* cartoon character Sylvester and the then U.S. President Bill Clinton's family cat Socks.

Williamina🐾

On account of our birds, cats were not allowed in the house; but from a friend in London I received a present of a white kitten, Williamina, and she and her numerous offspring had a happy home at "Gad's Hill". She became a favourite with all the household, and showed particular devotion to my father. I remember on one occasion when she had presented us with a family of kittens, she selected a corner of father's study for their home. She brought them one by one from the kitchen and deposited them in her chosen corner. My father called to me to remove them, saying that he could not allow the kittens to remain in his room. I did so, but Williamina brought them back again, one by one. Again they were removed. The third time, instead of putting them in the corner, she placed them all, and herself beside them, at my father's feet, and gave him such an imploring glance that he could resist no longer, and they were allowed to remain. As the kittens grew older they became more and more frolicsome, swarming up the curtains, playing about on the writing table and scampering behind the bookshelves. But they were never complained of and lived happily in the study until the time came for finding them other homes. One of these kittens was kept, who, as he was quite deaf, was left unnamed, and became known by servants as "the master's cat", because of his devotion to my father. He was always with him, and used to follow him about the garden like a dog, and sit with him while he wrote. One evening we were all, except father, going to a ball, and when we started, left "the master" and his cat in the drawing-room together. "The master" was reading at a small table, on which a lighted candle was placed. Suddenly the candle went out. My father, who was much interested in his book, relighted the candle, stroked the cat, who was looking at him pathetically he noticed, and continued his reading. A few minutes later, as the light became dim, he looked up just in time to see puss deliberately put out the candle with his paw, and then look appealingly towards him. This second and unmistakable hint was not disregarded, and puss was given the petting he craved. Father was full of this anecdote when all met at breakfast the next morning.

MAMIE DICKENS, *My Father as I Recall Him*, London: Roxburghe Press, 1896.

🐾The white cat (initially called William, but, following the above episode, there were no longer any doubts as to its gender) that the English writer Charles Dickens (1812–1870) chose as the "godfather" for his puppies.

Xena Hope, the cat who, every morning, waits for the St. Heliers Library in Auckland, New Zealand, to open and "helps children read." In 2012, her "office" (a colorful cat house) was stolen, shocking the community.

Xerxes, listed in the end credits as the feline that played the black cats in the horror/sci-fi movie *Monstrosity*, shown on television as *The Atomic Brain* (1963). In the film, an older woman hires a scientist to transplant her brain into a young woman's body. After experimenting with transplanting cat brains into human corpses and then the bodies of unfortunate lasses, the procedure is finalized, but the doctor decides to spare the chosen girl and instead transplants the brain of the elderly Mrs. March into a cat. Naturally, the cat/Mrs. March gets her revenge…

for *manX*

Aptly listed under the tail end of its name, this breed, which originated on the Isle of Man in the Irish Sea, is distinguished by the fact that it is tailless (due to a genetic mutation, although there are also several highly imaginative explanations as to why it has no tail).

Coat: short double coat as soft as that of a rabbit; it also has the latter's hopping gait
Temperament: "dog-like" (it follows its owner, digs holes and is affectionate) and a formidable mouse hunter

X for an (in)definite number⁕

"They began with four or five, and soon ran into double figures; there was a period within the writer's recollection when a visitor, on entering the sitting room, would experience the sensations of those defeated in a game of musical chairs; whichever he attempted to occupy, he found himself forestalled by a spreading matronly form, which proclaimed the imminence of yet another family."

This is how Francis Jekyll, nephew of Gertrude Jekyll, described the feline menagerie at his aunt's house in Surrey.

FRANCIS JEKYLL, *Gertrude Jekyll: A Memoir*, London: Jonathan Cape, 1934.

"One cat just leads to another... The place is so damned big it doesn't really seem as though there were many cats until you see them all moving like a mass migration at feeding time."

This is what Ernest Hemingway wrote in 1943 to his first wife (Hadley Richardson) from Cuba, where he was living with his third wife (Martha Gellhorn) and 11 cats. The number of cats grew to 23 with his fourth (and final) wife, Mary Welsh, at Finca Vigía, the author's home in Cuba. The "mass migration" numbered more than 50 at his home in Key West, Florida, where their descendants still live at the writer's residence, now converted into a museum.

HILARY HEMINGWAY, in CARLENE BRENNEN, *Hemingway's Cats: An Illustrated biography*, Sarasota, Florida: Pineapple Press, 2005, p. xii.

"Having a bunch of cats around is good. If you're feeling bad, you just look at the cats, you'll feel better, because they know everything is, just as it is. There's nothing to get excited about. They just know. They're saviors. The more cats you have, the longer you live. If you have a hundred cats, you'll live ten times longer than if you have ten. Someday this will be discovered, and people will have a thousand cats and live forever. It's truly ridiculous."

This is what CHARLES BUKOWSKI replied to SEAN PENN "on cats" in the interview "Tough Guys Write Poetry," *Interview Magazine*, September 1987.

Yellow Boy ("Marmaduke"), the combative long-haired orange cat of **Charles Henry Lane**, the nineteenth-century author of one of the first manuals on cat breeds (and more): *Rabbits, Cats and Cavies. Descriptive Sketches Of All Recognised Exhibition Varieties With Many Original Anecdotes* (1903). He was loving towards human beings, but less so towards fellow cats. "I was rather amused one day when I met one of my nearest neighbours, who owned a large short-haired tabby and white male, that had the reputation of being a 'bit of a boxer,' and he said to me, 'That yaller cat of yours is a hot 'un, and no mistake.' 'How so ?' I asked. 'Why,' he said, 'he came into our garden yesterday, and I'm blessed if he didn't pitch into our cat, and give him a downright good hiding, on his own ground—never seen such a thing in my life!' "I endeavoured to offer some apologies for the misdoings of my 'yaller cat,' but I firmly believe he had considerably raised himself in my neighbour's opinion by successfully carrying his warlike operations into the enemy's camp, and that his own cat, the larger and heavier animal, had gone down in his estimation at not being able to resist the daring intruder within his gates."
See also Laurel Queen and Victor

Misty Malarky Ying Yang, the Siamese cat of **Amy Carter**, daughter of former U.S. president Jimmy Carter (b. 1924), when the Carters lived in the White House.

Yum Yum, the inseparable Siamese companion of **Koko** in *The Cat Who…* series of mysteries written by **Lilian Jackson Braun** (1913–2011). "They were a pair of elegant Siamese whose seal-brown points were in striking contrast to their pale fawn bodies. The male, Kao K'o Kung, answered to the name of Koko; he was long, lithe, and muscular, and his fathomless blue eyes brimmed with intelligence. His female companion, Yum Yum, was small and delicate, with violet-blue eyes that could be large and heart-melting when she wanted to sit on a lap, yet that dainty creature could utter a piercing shriek when dinner was behind schedule."

Yule Cat (Jólakötturinn), the huge grimacing cat with razor-sharp whiskers who—according to Scandinavian legend—on Christmas Eve, devours children who are not wearing at least one new woolen garment. This less-than-festive fable stems from the importance of having completed work with the Fall wool before Yule, the reward for which was a new item of woolen clothing. Those who had not helped produce and process wool were subject to the cruelties of the Christmas cat.

Yvette, the Divine Yvette, a silver Persian who is the companion of **Midnight Louie** in the mystery novels by **Carole Nelson Douglas**.

for *York chocolate*

It was first bred in 1983 in New York State, the offspring of a long-haired cat with warm chocolate-brown coloring.

Coat: medium-long and silky, without an undercoat; solid chocolate or lilac, or bicolor with white

Temperament: referred to as a "satellite cat" because it tends to follow its human companion; shy towards strangers; loves to fall asleep on its owner's lap

Cat Y✤

In all my earlier years I used frequently to see my father come home in the dusk rather fagged with his round of teaching, and after dining he would lie down flat on the hearthrug close by the fire, and fall asleep for an hour or two, snoring vigorously. Beside him would stand up our old familiar tabby cat, poised on her haunches, and holding on by the fore-claws inserted into the fender-wires, warming her furry front. Her attitude (I have never seen any feline imitation of it) was peculiar, somewhat in the shape of a capital Y—"the cat making the Y" was my father's phrase for this performance.

Reference: William Michael Rossetti, *Dante Gabriel Rossetti. His Family Letters with a Memoir* (Volume One), London: Ellis & Elvey, 1895 (quoted in Christabel Aberconway (Baroness), *A Dictionary of Cat Lovers: XV Century B.C.–XX Century A.D.*, London: Michael Joseph, 1968 (1949), p. 318).

✤The otherwise anonymous tabby of Gabriele Rossetti (1783–1854), the Italian poet who emigrated to England and taught at King's College London and at King's College School. He was also the father of Cristina Rossetti, the poet, and of the Pre-Raphaelite painter Dante Gabriel Rossetti.

Zeris, *see Kerman*

Zézé, another name for "**Bourget**," the black cat of the French poet and playwright **François Édouard Joachim Coppée** (1842–1908). Bourget lived for more than 20 years and was a great fighter, as evidenced by his irregular ears.

See also Loulou

Zizi (1), the music-loving silver-grey Angora, and **Zuleika**, **Zulema** and **Zobeide**; just some of the many cats of **Théophile Gautier** (1811–72), French poet, novelist and critic.

See also Childebrand and Cléopâtre, Enjolras, Éponine (p. 30), Madame-Théophile (p. 62)

Zizi (2), the cat immortalized in the artwork of the French painter **Édouard Manet** (1832–83), such as *Woman with a Cat* (1880), which is currently in the National Gallery, London, on loan from the Tate.

Zombi, the "invisible" cat of Robert Southey (1774–1843), the English poet, man of letters and "philofelist." He was so named in reference to the leader (Zumbi) of the Quilombo dos Palmares, a community of escaped African slaves in Brazil, due to his dark, majestic appearance. As soon as he stepped into the house, however, the feline acted like a *zombie*, disappearing and showing himself just once after a horrific howl. Southey put forward the following hypotheses regarding this supernatural screeching, in a letter to Grosvenor Charles Bedford, Esq., April 3, 1821: "1. Had he seen the devil?
2. Was he making love to himself?
3. Was he engaged in single combat with himself?
5. Had he heard me sing, and was he attempting (vainly) to imitate it?"

See also Hurlyburlybuss, Ovid (p. 70) and Rumpelstilzchen

Zulu, one of the cats of the English physicist **Sir Oliver Lodge** (1851–1940). Miss Alney, Lodge's secretary, described the feline as follows: "At dinner when the Professor [Lodge] has finished the arduous work of the day, and at the end of the meal chats to his guests on outstanding human problems, or Relativity, or modern scientific ideas, Zulu is one of his most interested listeners. Should one of the guests interrupt, or cough, it is Zulu who looks up reproachfully, as if to say: 'Well, if he takes the trouble to explain things to you, at least you might listen. I shouldn't waste my time by telling you what I think about Relativity.'"

See also Oliver Twist and Nepia

Ziggy, an adventurous white cat who, on October 31, 2006, secretly boarded a ship at the Israeli port of Haifa, emerging from the container on November 17 when the vessel docked at Whitworth in Great Britain. He was more dead than alive, but was treated and adopted, and, because of his eyes—one green and one blue—he was named "Ziggy Stardust," after David Bowie's 1970s persona.

Zip-Zip, the Siamese of the American actress **Elizabeth Montgomery** (1933–95), who played Samantha in the television series *Bewitched*.

Zoë, the black-and-white cat of **Gabriele Rossetti** (1783–1854)—Italian poet, professor at King's College London and father of Christina and Dante Gabriel Rossetti—and daughter of the anonymous "cat Y" (*see* p. 110).

Zoe, the blind cat of **Neil Gaiman** (b. 1960), the English author who wrote the DC Comics series *The Sandman* and the award-winning *The Graveyard Book* (2008). "Zoe doesn't mew. She does a sort of a 'mwelp?' noise, as if she's talking to herself about things that puzzle her or that she's trying to remember. It's not very loud."

Zoroaster, one of the cats of the American writer **Mark Twain** (1835–1910). The author of *Adventures of Huckleberry Finn* (1884) shared a passion for cats with his scientist friend Nikola Tesla, and gave them bizarre names such as **Blatherskite** and **Sour Mash**. The exception is **Bambino**, a black kitten given to him by his daughter **Clara** (who had named the cat herself), to which Twain became quite attached. One evening, Bambino snuck off through a window, and Twain put ads in the local papers announcing a reward for his safe return. He was subsequently submerged with all sorts of cats—even after Bambino was found in the neighbor's yard three days later.

See also Apollinaris

Zula, the first known cat to be called an Abyssinian, supposedly "brought from Abyssinia at the conclusion of the war" to Great Britain in 1868 by Mrs. **Captain Barrett-Lennard**.

Zunar-J-5/9 Doric-4-7, *see Jake*

Zut, the leading character in a novella by the American humorist **Guy Wetmore Carryl** (1873–1904), *Zut and Others Parisians* (1903). The enormous white Angora belonged to the grocer Alexandrine Caille: "She had come into Alexandrine's possession as a kitten, and, what with much eating and an inherent dislike for exercise, had attained her present proportions and her superb air of unconcern. It was from the latter that she derived her name, the which, in Parisian argot, at once means everything and nothing, but is chiefly taken to signify complete and magnificent indifference to all things mundane and material: and in the matter of indifference Zut was past-mistress."

for *Zzzzzz*

Cats spend an astonishing amount of time sleeping: an average of 18 hours a day. This means that a 15-year-old cat has spent at least a decade sleeping! Like humans, cats also go through the REM sleep phase, which can easily be observed through the slight movements of their whiskers, paws and ears, and sometimes also vocalizations. But what they are dreaming of is a mystery, although it isn't hard to imagine… There are no known insomniac cats.

Zapaquilda ♟

Atop the tall roof ridge
sat beautiful Zapaquilda
licking herself from head to tail
in the cool breeze,
with a very serious and pompous air
as if she were a convent cat.

Her own thoughts
served as a mirror
even though a broken helmet
attracted a playful magpie
to which no cap or shawl
escaped as something to hide between those tiles,
near a doctor's attic.

…

Terrified, Zapaquilda ran away
through the attic, petticoat raised
(that which, for women, is an underskirt
of satin, cloth or shiny hoop,
for cats is a sinuous tail,
that bristles or curls *ad libitum*).

(Lope de Vega, *La Gatomaquia*, 1634)

REFERENCE: Tomé de Burguillos (pseud. Lope de Vega), *Rimas humanas y divinas del licenciado Tomé de Burguillos* (*Human and Divine Rhymes of Tomé de Burguillos, Esq.*), Madrid: A. Perez, 1634.

♟The *hermosa* (beautiful) cat whose graces are vied for by
Marramaquiz, a "*gato romano*" ("Roman cat"), and Micifuf,
"*Zapinarciso y Gatimarte*" (the "Narcissus and Mars" of
cats) in *La Gatomaquia*.

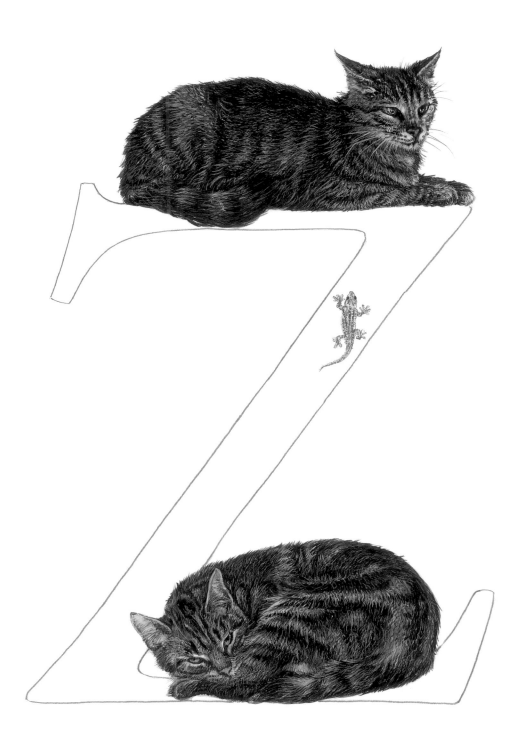

CHRISTABEL ABERCONWAY (Baroness), *A Dictionary of Cat Lovers: XV Century B.C.–XX Century A.D.*, London: Michael Joseph, 1968 (1949).

GEORG ADLER, PETER HUDIS & ANNELIES LASCHITZA (EDS.), *The Letters of Rosa Luxemburg*, London: Verso, 2011.

MARINA ALBERGHINI, *Jacopo Bassano (1510–1592) e il suo gatto*, Milan: Mursia, 1992.

MARINA ALBERGHINI, *Il gatto cosmico di Paul Klee*, Milan: Mursia, 1993.

MARINA ALBERGHINI, *Suzanne Valadon: L'amore felino*, Milan: Mursia, 1994.

MARINA ALBERGHINI, *Un gioiello per il re. La meravigliosa storia dell'angora bianco*, Milan: Mursia, 1995.

HANNAH ARENDT, *Men in Dark Times*, New York, NY: Harcourt, Brace and World, 1968.

STEPHEN ARTAULT DE VEVEY, "Des Actes Raisonnés chez le Chat," *Bulletin de l'Institut général psychologique*, 3(1), 1903: 13–14.

MARCEL AYMÉ, *Les contes du chat perché*, Paris: Gallimard, 1934–46.

WILLIAM BALDWIN, *A maruelous hystory intitulede, beware the Cat: Conteyning diuers wounderfull and incredible matters. Very pleasant and mery to read*, London: Wylliam Gryffith, 1570.

HONORÉ DE BALZAC, "Peines de cœur d'une chatte anglaise" ("Heartaches of an English Cat"), in *Scènes de la vie privée et publique des animaux* (*Public and private life of animals*), Paris: Flammarion, 1985 (first published, Paris: J. Hetzel & Paulin, 1842; also, J. Thomson (trans.), London: Sampson Low, Marston, Searle, & Rivington; Philadelphia, PA: J. B. Lippincott & Co., 1877).

CARLENE BRENNEN, *Hemingway's Cats: An Illustrated Biography*, Sarasota, FL: Pineapple Press, 2005.

CHARLES BUKOWSKI, *Women*, Santa Barbara, CA: Black Sparrow Press, 1978.

MIKHAIL BULGAKOV, *The Master and Margarita*, trans. M. Glenny, New York, NY: Harper & Row, 1967.

WILLIAM S. BURROUGHS, *The Cat Inside*, New York, NY: Grenfell Press, 1986.

BÉRÉNICE CAPATTI, *Klimt and his Cat*, Grand Rapids, MI: Eerdmans Books For Young Readers, 2004.

KAREL ČAPEK, *I Had a Dog and a Cat*, London: G. Allen & Unwin, 1940.

LEWIS CARROLL, *Alice's Adventures in Wonderland*, London: Macmillan & Co., 1865.

LOUIS-FERDINAND CÉLINE, *D'un château l'autre* (*Castle to Castle*), Paris: Gallimard, 1957; trans. R. Manheim, London: Blond, 1969.

LOUIS-FERDINAND CÉLINE, *Nord* (*North*), Paris: Gallimard, 1960; trans. R. Manheim, London: Bodley Head, 1972.

LOUIS-FERDINAND CÉLINE, *Rigodon* (*Rigadoon*), Paris: Gallimard, 1964; trans. R. Manheim, New York, NY: Delacorte Press, 1974.

SANDRA CHORON, HARRY CHORON & ARDEN MOORE, *Planet Cat: A Cat-alog*, Boston, MA: Houghton Mifflin, 2007.

COLETTE, *La Chatte*, Paris: B. Grasset, 1933. *See also* Willy.

JULIO CORTÁZAR, *Around the Day in Eighty Worlds*, trans. T. Christensen, San Francisco, CA: North Point Press, 1986.

PHILIP K. DICK, *Nick and the Glimmung*, London: Gollancz, 1988.

T.S. ELIOT, *Old Possum's Book of Practical Cats*, London: Faber & Faber, 1939.

ANATOLE FRANCE, *The Crime of Sylvestre Bonnard*, Paris: Calmann-Levy; trans. L. Hearn, London: James R. Osgood, 1891.

PAUL GALLICO, *Thomasina, The Cat Who Thought She Was God*, Garden City, NY: Doubleday, 1957.

THÉOPHILE GAUTIER, "My Private Menagerie," in *The Works of Théophile Gautier*, trans., ed. F. C. de Sumichrast, Cambridge, MA: Harvard University Press, 1902.

GORDON GORDON & MILDRED GORDON, *Undercover Cat*, Garden City, NY: Doubleday, 1963.

MARGHERITA HACK, *I gatti della mia vita*, illus. N. Costa, Trieste: Scienza Express, 2012.

ERNST HEMINGWAY, *Islands in the Stream*, New York, NY: Scribner, 1970.

PATRICIA HIGHSMITH, *The Animal Lover's Book of Beastly Murder*, New York, NY: Penzler Books, 1975.

E. T. A. HOFFMANN, *The Life and Opinions of the Tomcat Murr* (*Lebensansichten des Katers Murr*, 1820–22), trans. A. Bell, London: Penguin, 1999.

JORIS-KARL HUYSMANS, *En ménage*, Paris: G. Charpentier, 1881.

WASHINGTON IRVING, "Abbotsford and Newstead Abbey," in *The Crayon Miscellany*, Volume 2, Philadelphia: Carey, Lea & Blanchard, 1835.

JEAN-PIERRE JACKSON, *Les classiques du chat*, Paris: Coda, 2009.

LILIAN JACKSON BRAUN, *The Cat Who Could Read Backwards*, New York, NY: Dutton, 1966.

LILIAN JACKSON BRAUN, *The Cat Who Said Cheese*, New York, NY: Putnam, 1996.

JEROME K. JEROME, "On Cats and Dogs," in *Idle Thoughts of an Idle Fellow*, New York: Scribner & Welford, 1886.

STEPHEN KING, *Pet Sematary*, New York: Doubleday, 1983.

STEPHEN KING, *Sleepwalkers*, original screenplay, 6th draft, 1991 [unpublished], Columbia Pictures, 1992.

ERNEST LÉON LA JEUNESSE, *L'Inimitable*, Paris: Fasquelle, 1899.

CHARLES HENRY LANE, *Rabbits, Cats and Cavies. Descriptive Sketches Of All Recognised Exhibition Varieties With Many Original Anecdotes*, New York, NY: E.P. Dutton & Co., 1903. (The section concerning cats is available online at: http://www.messybeast.com/lane-cats.htm.)

ROBERT DE LAROCHE, *L'Enchatclopédie*, Paris: L'Archipel, 2010.

Bibliography

DORIS LESSING, *Particularly Cats… and Rufus*, New York, NY: Knopf, 1991; rev. ed. *Particularly Cats: including the essays "Rufus, the Survivor" and "The Old Age of El Magnifico,"* Short Hills, NJ: Burford Books, 1993.

PIERRE LOTI, *Lives of Two Cats*, trans. M. B. Richards, Boston, MA: Riverside Press, 1900.

HOWARD P. LOVECRAFT, "Cats and Dogs," in *Something About Cats and Other Pieces*, Sauk City, WI: Arkham House, 1949.

DIANE LOVEJOY, *Cat Lady Chronicles*, Milan: Officina Libraria, 2012.

MOIRA MEIGHN, *Children of the Moon. A Booklet Concerning Cats*, London: Medici Society, 1929.

P. I. MALTBIE, *Picasso and Minou*, illus. P. Estrada, Watertown, MA: Charlesbridge, 2005.

SIR PATRICK MOORE, *Miaow!: Cats Really Are Nicer than People*, Dorchester: Hubble & Hattie, 2012.

DANIELE MORANTE (ed.) (with GIULIANA ZAGRA), *L'amata: Lettere di e a Elsa Morante*, Turin: Einaudi, 2012.

VICKI MYRON & BRET WITTER, *Dewey: The Small-Town Library Cat Who Touched the World*, New York, NY: Grand Central Publishing, 2008.

CAROLE NELSON DOUGLAS, *Catnap: A Midnight Louie Mystery*, New York: Tor, 1992.

CAROLE NELSON DOUGLAS, *Pussyfoot: A Midnight Louie Mystery*, New York: Tor, 1993.

CAROLE NELSON DOUGLAS, *Cat in a Neon Nightmare*, New York, NY: Forge, 2004.

MICHAEL NEWMAN, W. H. AUDEN, "The Art of Poetry No. 17," in *Paris Review*, 57, Spring 1974.

FRANCINE PATTERSON, *Koko's Kitten*, New York, NY: Scholastic, 1985.

MARIA TERESA JEANNE PEREGO, *Joseph and Chico: The Life of Pope Benedict XVI as Told by a Cat*, San Francisco, CA: Ignatius Press, 2008.

CHARLES PERRAULT, "Le Chat Bott" ("Puss in Boots"), in *Puss in Boots and Diamonds and Toads: Tales for the Nursery*, 6th ed., trans., London: Printed for Tabart & Co., 1804.

ELIZABETH PETERS, *The Curse of the Pharaohs*, New York, NY: Dodd, Mead, 1981.

ELIZABETH PETERS, *The Snake, the Crocodile, and the Dog*, New York, NY: Warner Books, 1992.

EDGAR ALLAN POE, "The Black Cat," in *Tales*, New York, NY: Wiley and Putnam, 1845.

AGNES REPPLIER, *The Fireside Sphinx*, Boston, MA: Houghton, Mifflin & Co., 1901.

NIKOLAY RIMSKY-KORSAKOV, NADEAHDA NIKOLAEVNA RIMSKAIA-KORSAKOSA, YEHUDAH YOFE & CARL VAN VECHTEN (EDS.), *My Musical Life*, New York, NY: A. A. Knopf, 1923; in Russian, *Letopis' moeĭ muzykal›noĭ zhizni*, 1844–1906, St. Petersburg: Tip. Glazunova, 1909.

SAKI (Hector Hugh Munro), "The Reticence of Lady Anne," in *Reginald in Russia and Other Sketches*, London: Methuen & Co., 1910.

SAKI (Hector Hugh Munro), *The Chronicles of Clovis*, New York, NY: Viking Press, 1911.

S. F. SAID, *Varjak Paw*, New York, NY: David Flickling Books, 2003.

MICHÈLE SACQUIN, *The Well-Read Cat*, trans. I. Ollivier, Milan, Paris: Officina Libraria, Bibliothèque nationale de France, 2010.

ARNOLD HENRY SAVAGE LANDOR, *Across Coveted Lands*, vol. 2, London: Macmillan & Co., 1902.

JOSEPH VICTOR VON SCHEFFEL, *Der Trompeter von Säkkingen: ein sang vom Oberrhein*, Leipzig: J. Schuberth & C., 1884.

BARBARA SLEIGH, *Carbonel: the King of Cats*, London: Puffin Books, 1955.

YVONNE SKARGON, *The Importance of Being Oscar*, Swavesey, Cambridge: Silent Books, 1988.

YVONNE SKARGON, *Lily & Hodge & Dr Johnson*, Swavesey, Cambridge: Silent Books, 1991.

SAM STALL, *100 Cats Who Changed Civilization: History's Most Influential Felines*, Philadelphia, PA: Quirk Books, 2007.

LUDWIG TIECK, *Der gestiefelte Kater: ein Kindermärchen in drey Akten mit Zwischenspielen, einem Prologe und Epiloge*, Bergamo: Auf Kosten des Verfassers, 1797; *Der gestiefelte Kater (Puss in Boots)*, trans. G. Gillespie, Edinburgh: Edinburgh University Press, 1974.

MARK TWAIN, *Roughing It*, Hartford, CN: American Publishing Company, 1872.

PIETRO DELLA VALLE, *Viaggi di Pietro della Valle il pellegrino: descritti da lui medesimo in lettere familiari all'erudito suo amico Mario Schipano. La Persia. Parte seconda (The Travels of Pietro della Valle, the Pilgrim: Described in Private Letters to the Scholar and his Friend Mario Schipano. Persia, Part Two)*, Rome: 1658.

CARL VAN VECHTEN, *The Tiger in the House*, New York, NY: A. A. Knopf, 1920.

ROY VICKERS, "Miss Paisley's Cat," in *Best Police Stories*, London: Faber & Faber, 1966.

FRÉDÉRIC VITOUX, *Bébert: Le chat de Louis-Ferdinand Céline*, Paris: B. Grasset, 1976.

CHARLES DUDLEY WARNER, "Calvin (A Study of Character)," in *My Summer in a Garden*, Boston, MA: James R. Osgood, 1873.

ANDREW LLOYD WEBBER & JOHN NAPIER, *Cats: The Book of the Musical, Based on "Old Possum's Book of Practical Cats" by T. S. Eliot*, New York, NY: Harcourt Brace Jovanovich, 1983.

WILLY [Colette], *Claudine à l'école*, Paris: P. Ollendorff, 1900.

WILLY [Colette], *Claudine à Paris*, Paris: P. Ollendorff, 1901; *Claudine in Paris*, trans. A. White, New York, NY: Farrar, Straus and Cudahy, 1958.

WILLY [Colette], *Sept dialogues de bêtes*, Paris: Société du Mercure de France, 1905.

Delilah, Oscar, Tiffany… and many more of Freddie Mercury's cats
www.freddie.ru/e/cats

Dewey Readmore Books, Nyx and Xena—library cats
www.deweyreadmorebooks.com
www.overbooked.com/nyx
http://twitter.com/xenathecat

Elvis, Salt and Pepper… and many more of John Lennon's cats
www.catanna.com/johnlennonscats.htm

Hamlet and Matilda, the Algonquin Hotel's "most famous guests"
www.algonquinhotel.com/algonquin-cat

Grumpy Cat, "the world's grumpiest cat"
www.grumpycats.com

Henri (Le Chat Noir), "the world's first and foremost feline philosopher"
www.henrilechatnoir.com

Huan and Jerry appear to answer the question: Do Cats Really Love Mice?
www.youtube.com/watch?v=WyM2r-ixDvg

Jock, Nelson, Tango… and others in Sir Winston Churchill's feline menagerie
www.winstonchurchill.org/support/the-churchill-centre/publications/finest-hour/
issues-109-to-144/no-139/837-churchills-feline-menagerie

Kai, being sung to by Patti Smith
www.youtube.com/watch?v=NV2-IZFgH2U

Lil Bub, "the most amazing cat on the planet"
http://lilbub.com

New Boy, Poo Jones… and other cats of Vivien Leigh
www.anothermag.com/current/view/1290/Vivien_Leighs_Cats

Nora, the piano cat
www.norathepianocat.com

Websites

Socks, a former First Cat
http://presidentialpetmuseum.com/pets/socks/

Ulric and the PDSA (People's Dispensary for Sick Animals) Pet Fit Club
www.pdsa.org.uk/pet-health-advice/pdsa-pet-fit-club/ulric

Cats and artists
www.rotorama.com/famous-artists-and-their-cats/

Cats as artists
www.monpa.com

Cats in cartoons
www.simonscat.com/
muttscomics.com/default.aspx

Cats in history (and other famous felines)
www.purr-n-fur.org.uk

Cats in movies
http://catsonfilm.wordpress.com

Cats in museums
www.hemingwayhome.com/cats/
www.youtube.com/watch?v=LaTU93l4dmA

Cats and writers
http://catladiesproject.blogspot.co.uk/search/label/Cat%20People
http://weimarart.blogspot.com/2011/05/literate-cat.html
www.album.aufeminin.com/album/818604/chats-d-ecrivains-19594467.html#p1
www.mentalfloss.com/article/49302/11-writers-who-really-loved-cats
www.buzzfeed.com/summeranne/30-renowned-authors-inspired-by-cats

My Baby Just Cares for Me by Nina Simone—Aardman Animations video
www.youtube.com/watch?v=eYSbUOoq4Vg

The Rabbi's Cat (2012)
https://www.youtube.com/watch?v=F6nyQiu5nzE

Residents and visitors

Padam (the Secretary) is the Alpha Cat of Officina Libraria, a majestic but slightly overweight tabby with emerald eyes. He owes his name to a song by Edith Piaf that goes: "Padam ... padam ... padam ... / Il arrive en courant derrière moi". Precisely… from the time he was a kitten, six years ago, every day he has come to the office, serving as… a paperweight. He has his own desk, but doesn't disregard cardboard boxes or the executive armchair. One of his other duties is to stimulate the publishers to exercise, forcing them to get up even ten times a day to refill his bowl (their punishment being harm to people and things). He loves to receive visiting authors, particularly if they arrive with bags or backpacks, and—*ça va sans dire*—he is mad about bookcases, as he loves clamber to the top shelf.

Inutil (Inutillo), a black stray cat with a white patch under his neck and another on the tip of his tail. One October day, we found him in the middle of the street, where he had stretched out, perhaps hoping to get hit by a car. Although he was an adult male, he weighed just 6 pounds and had more fleas than fur. Well fed and well taken care of, he spent the last year of his life coddled and loved, and was never stingy with his purring.

Birba, the calico cat on the cover of the Italian edition of this book. She fell in love with **Padam** (employing the rather aggressive manner of children who lash out to show their love), and started to visit him more and more. In the end, she decided to leave her own home and "adopt" Padam's—and, of course, Officina's headquarters. She spends most of the day wandering around our district, taking advantage of the comings and goings of our neighbors (all of whom know her) then shows up at our door, usually for an extra breakfast, sometimes for lunch and always for an afternoon snack. Then she hangs around until we call it a day and she returns home with Padam.

Quazzo, the bellicose tabby that got himself adopted by me (Paola Gallerani) while writing this book. He owes his name to my friend and business partner, Marco Jellinek. Me: "Marco, we haven't got any cats starting with 'Q.'" Marco: "Quazzo." [A word not entirely dissimilar to another, somewhat ruder, exclamatory word in Italian!] Two days later… well, this happened: "There. Not even three months of solitude and freedom, and he arrived… I had sworn I wouldn't fall for it again, at least not this fast, and in any case I wanted a different type, perhaps with blue eyes… black hair would have been fine… but mainly the kind that seeks you out and makes you feel like they really care. I didn't expect to meet—and certainly didn't seek—the usual ordinary male: young and athletic, of course, but one of those living day to day, following the distraction of the moment. Probably unreliable and moody. But it took just one look, when his light golden eyes locked with mine just an instant too long, and he rubbed past me… When a cat chooses you, there's no escape. Quazzo." (*Giornale balsamico*, July 3, 2013)

The Cats

of the Officina

Associates

Sasso, aka "Ji, the world's most beautiful cat," is Marco Jellinek's big white feline roommate. The whiteness of his coat is a congenital anomaly that also causes deafness. In turn, this deafness is responsible for his incredibly loud mewing in the middle of the night to convince Marco to open the window so he can go outside… and then come back in (in fact, the window is always open). We have no clue why he is so terrified when guests come to visit, but one thing is sure: He scampers off as fast as lightning.

Indy and Minny, the cats of Serena Solla. Indy was named after Indiana Jones, because, as a kitten, he would constantly jump and run all over the house, even at night (and over the slumbering bodies of Serena's family). Now that he is an ultra-centenarian (in cat years), he has calmed down, and his movements are limited to a couple of slow strolls towards his food, the litter box or—when he is in fine form—the lounge chair on the balcony. Minerva, nicknamed Minny, was found in the Romagna countryside when she was just a few days old, and her character is typical of that area. She never lets anyone step on her toes—um, paws—but she can also be utterly generous and affectionate right down to the tip of her tail… when she wants to be stroked. Although she has now grown quite a bit (particularly in girth), she nonetheless thinks she's still little and manages to squirm through every crack and cubbyhole in the house, forcing the family to embark on impromptu "treasure hunts" to find her.

Clary and Sage, tortoiseshell-and-white sisters named after an aromatherapy herb that purports to focus the mind—not so, sadly, in its feline form, as Kim Yarwood can attest even as recently as during the course of working on this very book…

for *gatto Padam*

Gabriella Gallerani lives and works in Milan with Pedro, the yellow-headed Amazon parrot and percussionist, and York (Pocio), the inseparable Yorkshire terrier with every trait of a Yorkie except temperament and size. But there is an endless list of pets that have been part of her life throughout her career as an illustrator, working on publications such as the *Guide alla natura d'Italia* (Mondadori, 1969–80), magazines such as *Gardenia* and *Giardini*, and including the recent *trompe-l'oeil* bags in wood and silk. She has painted these animals hair by hair, feather by feather and scale by scale, with the results that they look even more realistic than the flesh-and-blood pets. www.gabriellagallerani.it

Paola Gallerani lives and works in Milan and Paris (and has always dreamed of writing that) with her cat Quazzo. In one of her other nine lives, she was an art historian, but is now a publisher, art director and sometimes author for Officina Libraria. The desk where Padam and Birba take turns dozing is hers. www.lo-ed.com/amelie-paola-gallerani

Other books about cats published by Officina Libraria:
Michèle Sacquin, *The Well-Read Cat*, Milan: Officina Libraria, 2010
Diane Lovejoy, *Cat Lady Chronicles* (with ten cats illustrated by Gabriella Gallerani), Milan: Officina Libraria, 2012

Other books (not about cats) by Paola Gallerani:
(as Paola Gallerani)
Questo quaderno appartiene a Giovanni Testori, Inediti dall'Archivio, Milan: Officina Libraria, 2007
The Menagerie of Pieter Boel: Animal Painter in the Age of Louis XIV, Milan: Officina Libraria, 2012

(as Amélie Galé, with illustrations by Jack Tow)
The Sforza Castle, Milan: Officina Libraria, 2007
Up All Night with Howie, Milan: LO editions, 2012
Who's Afraid of Howie?, Milan: LO editions, 2013

FSC
www.fsc.org

MIX
Paper from
responsible sources
FSC® C013123

Typeset in Adobe Garamond and printed on 150 g Gardapat Kiara.
Printed in Italy by Graphicom, Vicenza, in December 2013
ex Officina Libraria Jellinek et Gallerani